Developments in Intellectual Property Strategy

"This is a fascinating book that provides its readers with a comprehensive interdisciplinary journey to addressing unpacking intellectual property, ethical and governance challenges while frontier technologies are engaged, as well as exploring responding strategies to the business world. It is an impressive reading book for academic scholars, business professionals, industry practitioners and policymakers."

—Dr Luo Li, *Assistant Professor of Law, Coventry Law School, Coventry University, UK*

"Dr. Nadia has put out an awesome literature, which is relevant not just for academics, but it is for all cadre of society. Her interdisciplinary and cross-cultural approaches to the treatment of the evolving issues surrounding artificial intelligence (AI) is uniquely presented in this work: 'Developments in Intellectual Property Strategy: The Impact of Artificial Intelligence, Robotics and New Technologies.' I highly recommend this book to anyone engaged in the economics, politics, legal, and technology spaces."

—Professor Samuel Samiái Andrews, *USA Ambassador's Distinguished Scholar, Professor of Intellectual Property Law & faculty, member, Prince Mohammad Bin Fahd University, College of Law, Al Khobar, Kingdom of Saudi Arabia*

Nadia Naim
Editor

Developments in Intellectual Property Strategy

The Impact of Artificial Intelligence, Robotics and New Technologies

palgrave
macmillan

Editor
Nadia Naim
Law and Social Sciences
Aston University
Birmingham, UK

ISBN 978-3-031-42575-2 ISBN 978-3-031-42576-9 (eBook)
https://doi.org/10.1007/978-3-031-42576-9

This Palgrave Macmillan imprint is published by the registered company Springer Nature Switzerland AG.
The registered company address is: Gewerbestrasse 11, 6330 Cham, Switzerland

Paper in this product is recyclable.

Foreword

The contemporary debates that currently rage in academe and social media on the nature and merits or otherwise of new technologies, artificial Intelligence and robotics at times encompass a spectrum ranging from predictions of a society of positive performance where mankind's contribution to climatic chaos is under control, menial labour is performed by machines, poverty and pandemic no longer prevail, to a robotic-ruled regime and even to the eventual end of mankind as we know it and think we understand it today.

So sound and reasoned analysis of key elements of the interaction of intellectual property and its societal and business engagement now and in any future are at times overlooked in these ranging exchanges.

Dr Nadia Naim endeavours, very successfully in this writer's humble view, to introduce much-needed balance in addressing some of these key elements. Nadia is well qualified to so examine these elements, having researched and published widely in the field of intellectual property rights and protection regimes in domestic, regional and broader international contexts. Her most recent publication, for example, has examined Islamic legal principles and intellectual property rights in the member states of the Arabian Gulf states.

This latest book offers chapters by Nadia and a number of expert contributors whose analyses encompass both fundamentals and crucial areas that are often overlooked or do not receive the deserved attention they warrant in the raging exchanges over future projections on society and business. The impact of emerging and future technologies upon society and its relationship between established current intellectual property rights protection regimes and the new technologies like artificial intelligence require a sound and balanced contribution to tempering discourses coloured by speculation and emotion. This book sets out to achieve that high aspiration. It covers core topics such as artificial intelligence creations and ownership—who can, and should, own the intellectual property that artificial intelligence, as distinct from natural person or legal entity, might create?—which in itself require examination of the regulation and/or protection of intellectual property creativity or invention conceived by artificial intelligence or protection and whether such issues are just a matter of time or a step too far. Irrespective of that response, society and business are already confronted with the challenge of the big data and the risk of data legislation such as the EU Data Act and comparable UK statutes enshrining quasi-exclusivity data lockups. The legal nature of non-fungible tokens, utilising the exemplar of trade in artworks in the digital environment, also receives attention, as does the potential for robots to adopt a role as care contributors in the ever-increasing and concerning industry of proper and appropriate attention to our ageing population in care. Finally, the book offers perspectives on the value of intellectual property financing for companies and businesses, and an examination of transformative (bio)technologies in knowledge societies.

Nadia and her co-contributors bring a fresh and essential critical analysis to the debate on these legal and regulatory considerations of intellectual rights and artificial intelligence within society and the business world. This book covers a broad yet manageable array of topics, some of which are otherwise overlooked, on the future of business intellectual property strategy and planning, with a comprehensive interdisciplinary review of the rapidly evolving fields of artificial intelligence and consequent new technologies. It is a welcome contribution and advance to the current debate.

It will be enjoyed by scholars and practitioners alike, as well as by those generally of enquiring mind.

Emeritus Professor International Law
School of Law, Faculty of Arts and Society
Charles Darwin University
Darwin, Australia

David Price

Preface

Developments in intellectual property strategy is a cutting-edge and business-focussed publication on the impact of IP in the business world. Taking an interdisciplinary and diverse perspective, this book enriches the evolving definition and scope of intellectual property and the impact of artificial intelligence, robotics and new technologies literature by focusing on actors, products and regulation that shape the business sector. Considering the gap between theory and practice, this book bridges academic and professional knowledge in unpacking legal, ethical and governance issues in the intellectual property industry. In an effort to include as many viewpoints as possible, regardless of popularity or who holds them, the book editor gathered thoughts from diverse fields, including business, intellectual property, artificial intelligence, ethics, governance, law and management. Appealing to academic stakeholders with an interest in international intellectual property developments and the impact of emerging technologies, this book is the result of and a testament to a distinct educational project that includes different countries and communities for future reference.

The book aims to develop an understanding of the legal challenges posed by intellectual property, artificial intelligence and robotics technologies, along with a consideration of appropriate business and regulatory responses. It provides a business-focussed framework for considering concepts and principles that relate to the development and use of such technologies. It considers different legal and regulatory governance regimes at the international, regional and national levels. It explores the application and impact of artificial intelligence and intellectual property in the current Industrial 4.0 revolution era. For artificial intelligence, scenarios such as automated and algorithmic decision-making in business and finance, ageing population and healthcare robots will be discussed.

From the intellectual property angle, the book will examine the protection of the intangible but marketable proprietary interests related to goodwill, trademarks, trade and personal secrets, know-how and inventions. In addition it will also examine the protection given to literary, artistic and musical creations; the products of music recording, film, broadcasting and other media companies; and designs used in commercial and industrial spheres. This will include the protection given by UK and EU law and international conventions. The increasing importance of such law in the modern business environment, the protection of biotechnological invention and the impact of the digital environment will be emphasised. The book will develop a critical awareness of the nature of the issues surrounding intellectual property rights and the role they play in the business world. For intellectual property, the chapters will also cover the value of intellectual property audits for companies, balancing the need for growth in enterprise and innovation.

The book aims to provide an intellectually stimulating and practically engaging approach to address legal and ethical issues relating to artificial intelligence and intellectual property; in particular, Chap. 1 considers different legal and regulatory governance regimes at the international, regional and national levels. Currently, all intellectual property rights created with human and artificial intelligence "effort" belong to the human owner; however, as artificial intelligence becomes more sophisticated, the law on intellectual property protection will need to adapt accordingly.

Chapter 2 considers the legal and ethical questions concerning the generation and utilisation of big data; the traditional legal distinction between online-offline issues is not sufficient to deal with the intricacies of big data, AI and smart technologies and the specialised laws and regulations will be examined on how to regulate issues in specific fields.

Chapter 3 explores the legal nature of non-fungible tokens (NFTs) and what rights and interests purchasers acquire. It contextualises the discussion against the background of the trade of artworks in a blockchain environment; examines the most recent legislation and court decisions concerning NFTs and cryptocurrency; and conducts a comparative study between the selected common law and civil law systems on their concept of assets and property in relation to NFTs.

Chapter 4 aims to discuss the involvement of artificial intelligence in the intellectual property value chain, beyond the earlier questions in the book on artificial intelligence as a creator/inventor but also the role of artificial intelligence as a user of protected intangible assets. The challenges are discussed with respect to two areas of intellectual property: copyright and patents. There is an in-depth analysis of the DABUS case and the various judgements in the UK, USA, Germany, South Africa and Australia.

Expanding further on the theme of artificial intelligence and intellectual property and more specifically on patent law, Chap. 5 discusses the emerging issues of artificial intelligence in countries beyond those considered in the earlier chapters. Focussing on Indonesian patent law, which currently does not include provisions for artificial intelligence inventions, the analysis highlights the problem in the protection of artificial intelligence inventions, with a deeper study into understanding artificial intelligence inventions and Indonesian patent law. A comparison of studies in Indonesian and Japanese patent laws on artificial intelligence inventions is conducted to find similarities and differences between the two countries regarding the protection of artificial intelligence inventions.

Ageing population and healthcare robots are the focus of Chap. 6. Scientific progress in robotics, artificial intelligence integrated systems and increasingly sophisticated software engineering has contributed to innovative developments in care robots in the Asia Pacific regions, Europe and the USA. Whilst the use of care robots is not widespread, research is already occurring to integrate wider use of care robots in the elderly population towards improving their quality of life. Developments in care robots for the elderly are valuable, yet they give rise to special concerns as they affect peoples' health and safety. Key ethical and legal issues arising from the use of care robots in the ageing population such as deception and trust from care robots are highlighted, which implicate governance concerns ranging from balancing innovations and ensuring user safety to determining the appropriate levels of regulatory oversight and support for developers and market strategies. An examination of these issues provides some guidance for law makers and policy developers in these areas of concern.

An examination of the tangible value of IP financing for companies and businesses lends weight to the overall vision of the book to weigh in on the impact of artificial intelligence on intellectual property strategy; as in a nutshell, the artificial intelligence world wants a slice of the intellectual property pie. Intangible assets are today recognised by many companies as their most important resource. Without intellectual property rights, many innovative ventures have nothing to sell or licence. In contemporary knowledge-intensive economies, from the world's largest and most powerful companies to the smallest small- to medium-sized enterprises, the exploitation of intellectual assets—copyright, patents, trademarks, designs and know-how—is essential to business and the creative industries. However intellectual property is rarely sufficient, of itself, to create businesses or, indeed, to create significant economic value; it needs to be incorporated into a commercialisation plan. A successful future for intellectual property financing is a significant step in further development of the potential for an intellectual property and artificial intelligence-based economy.

Chapter 8 aims to gain a better understanding of "knowledge society" epistemologies and explore the role of patents in cellular agriculture, a field of enquiry that uses cell-cultivation technology, as a case study to elucidate the extent to which intellectual property rights can be deployed to generate optimal public welfare. Through a public interest lens, it also seeks to understand whether growing calls for open science can be aligned with the needs of a flourishing innovation ecosystem. Combining theoretical and doctrinal legal approaches along with insights from political and economic theories on regulation and governance, the final chapter looks at some of the legal questions to illuminate how governments, regulators and stakeholders balance and meet the demands of pressing social challenges, such as climate change and food insecurity, with the benefits of transformative biotechnologies to create intellectual commons.

Birmingham, UK Nadia Naim

Contents

Notes on Contributors

Arianna Alpini is Associate Professor of Private Law in the Department of Law at the University of Macerata, Italy, where she lectures on private law and sport law. She also teaches foundations of private law in the European and Comparative Legal Studies international degree programme. She was Assistant Professor of Private Law and Adjunct Professor of Legal Method at University of Sannio, Italy. She is a fellow of the European Law Institute (ELI) and a member of the Italian Association of Civil Law Scholars (SISDiC). Her research interests include the impact of technologies on contract law. She is an author of monographs, essays, articles and notes on obligations, co-ownership, European principles, interpretation and sources of law and fundamental rights protection. She is the principal investigator in a research project on transdisciplinary methodology, and the coordinator of a research unit on consumer protection.

Muralidharan Anantharaman graduated from National University of Singapore (NUS) with a BSc in Life Sciences in 2010 and then an MA in Philosophy in 2014. In 2014 and 2015 he was a teaching assistant in the Department of Philosophy and a research assistant at the Centre for Biomedical Ethics; he holds a PhD in Philosophy from the University of Warwick, UK. After graduating in 2020, he became a lecturer at Singapore University of Social Sciences (SUSS), before re-joining the Centre as a research fellow in 2021. He has research interests in political philosophy, epistemology as well as normative and applied ethics.

Hui Yun Chan is a Research Fellow in the Yong Loo Lin School of Medicine at the Centre for Biomedical Ethics, National University of Singapore, Singapore. Hui Yun has held several law lectureships in universities in the UK and is a fellow of the Higher Education Academy, UK. She has written scholarly articles in the fields of bioethics and health law on topics in healthcare decision-making law and ethics, organ donation, and a monograph on advance healthcare decision-making titled *Advance Directives: Rethinking Regulation, Autonomy and Healthcare Decision-Making* (2018). She has written about the legal and ethical aspects of COVID-19 related issues, and public health regulation and ethics.

Mariela de Amstalden's research explores the legal implications of emerging biotechnologies, in particular animal cell cultivation, and their implications for international economic law and global governance. Her monograph, *Global Food Governance: Implications of Food Safety and Quality Standards in International Trade Law* (Berne, 2015), explores how the notion of legal standards in international law can be interpreted to ensure that global food demands are met. She has experience in private practice and the judiciary and has written a number of peer-reviewed articles about the law of emerging biotechnologies, food and public health regulation at the intersection with international economic law and global governance.

Lucius Klobucnik is Lecturer in Intellectual Property Law at Aston University, Birmingham, UK. He holds a PhD degree from Queen Mary University, London, and Max Planck Institute for Innovation and Competition in Munich (Augsburg University). His main research focuses on copyright law (especially music rights), intellectual property in new technologies and platform liability. As part of his PhD research project, he worked at the German Collective Management Organisation in Music Rights (GEMA) in Munich, and at CISAC (Confederation of Societies of Authors and Composers) in Paris.

Galih Dwi Ramadhan is a lecturer at the Faculty of Law, Universitas Islam Indonesia (FH UII), having joined in early 2024. His primary legal expertise lies in Intellectual Property Rights and Internet Law. He holds Master of Law degrees (LL.M. from Youngsan University, South Korea, and M.H. from UII, 2022). His current research focuses on IP issues in traditional and popular culture, and legal implications of Internet of Things (IoT) technology.

Nadia Naim is Associate Dean for Internationalisation and Senior Lecturer in Law at Aston University, UK. She is a qualified barrister and fellow of the Higher Education Academy. She has written many scholarly articles in the areas of international intellectual property law, intangible asset financing and development, comparative law, Islamic law and international law. She has authored books in the intellectual property field and specialises in emerging areas of intellectual property and value-based financing development.

Budi Agus Riswandi is Professor of Law in the field of intellectual property rights and cyberlaw and a dean of the Faculty of Law, Universitas Islam Indonesia, Indonesia. He teaches intellectual property law at the Faculty of Law, Universitas Islam Indonesia. In addition, he also teaches at various law faculties in Indonesia. He usually conducts research focusing on the field of intellectual property rights and cyberlaw and publications in the form of books and journals in the field of intellectual property rights and cyberlaw. He is also usually appointed as a speaker in various scientific activities such as seminars or conferences both at national and at international levels, especially in the field of intellectual property rights and cyberlaw. He is also registered as an advocate with the Indonesian Advocates Association and a registered Intellectual Property Consultant at the Directorate General of Intellectual Property of the Ministry of Law and Human Rights of the Republic of Indonesia as well as the Coordinator of the Intellectual Property Consultants Association of Yogyakarta Special Region. In addition, he is also the Chairman of the Indonesian Intellectual Property Centre Association.

Marc A. Stuhldreier is a Postdoctoral Fellow at Linköping University, Sweden, in the ERC-funded PASSIM project. He is a qualified data protection officer and auditor in Germany. His research focusses on the intersection between intellectual property rights and human rights, with a particular focus on the impacts of private exclusive rights on public access. Focussing on the accessibility of medicines in much of his works, he further addresses new related issues stemming from currently debated data regulations and their anticipated impact on future public research and innovation.

Nivita Sukhadia holds a LLB in Law with Business Studies graduate from the University of Birmingham, UK, and is also a Master of Law student at the University of Cambridge. She works as a part-time research assistant in the intellectual property law field.

Angelia Jia Wang is an assistant professor in the Law School at Durham University, UK. Prior to joining Durham Law School in 2020, she taught at the Hong Kong Polytechnic University. She has been a Research Fellow at the Berkman Center for Internet and Society (now the Berkman Klein Centre), Harvard University, and a Postdoc Fellow at the Law School, Singapore Management University. Her research interests lie in the areas of intellectual property law and the intersection between law and technology. Her recent research projects include intellectual property law (IP) and artificial intelligence, IP and video games and IP for tokenised artwork. Her work is published in *European Intellectual Property Review*, *Intellectual Property Law & Practice*, *Hong Kong Law Journal*, *European Review of Private Law* and *Asian Pacific Law Review*, and she has also written a monograph.

Artificial Intelligence Creations and Ownership – Who Should the Intellectual Property Belong To?

Nadia Naim

Research in this area enters the rapidly growing artificial intelligence and robotics industries in the legal, business, manufacturing, and healthcare sectors and the impact of intellectual property protection on emerging technologies. This chapter aims to develop an understanding of the legal and ethical challenges posed by artificial intelligence and robotics technologies, along with consideration of appropriate legal and regulatory responses. It provides a philosophical and legal framework for considering concepts and principles that relate to the development and use of such technologies. It considers different legal and regulatory governance regimes at the international, regional, and national levels. Currently, all intellectual property rights created with human and artificial intelligence "effort", belong to the human however as artificial intelligence becomes more sophisticated, the law on intellectual property protection will need to adapt accordingly. The chapter will focus on the interplay between

N. Naim (✉)
Law and Social Sciences, Aston University, Birmingham, UK
e-mail: n.naim@aston.ac.uk

N. Naim (ed.), *Developments in Intellectual Property Strategy*,
https://doi.org/10.1007/978-3-031-42576-9_1

intellectual property and artificial intelligence, intellectual property rights protection affords the human intellectual property rights holder a time-limited monopoly over their intangible asset and has yet to afford any mirror rights or alternative rights to artificial intelligence.

At present, artificial intelligence can be seen to adequately respond to humans' needs, such as virtual digital assistance, most people will have Apple Siri, Alexa and or Google Home, that respond using voice recognition systems. Many rely on artificial intelligence to provide a recommended list of music based on your existing music choices and preferences, and produce works of art (Li 2020). Most notably, a project team behind The Next Rembrandt designed algorithms that allowed a computer to create a painting in the style of the seventeenth century Dutch artist and is known as the Rembrandt 2.0. Artificial intelligence can produce works which could be considered as copyright works however the law has yet to acknowledge AI as a copyright owner. Humans working in creative, innovative and legal sectors are discussing the consequence of AI systems when it comes to who will own the intellectual property, more importantly, who will the economic rights belong to. Artificial intelligence systems are developing at a significant pace and as a result, reshaping the whole creative and innovative sectors that are protected in the existing intellectual property system. Therefore, it is necessary to identify the AI systems at present, defining and distinguishing between the concepts of "AI-assisted" and "AI-generated", to outline the direction of AI development in the context of intellectual property law.

Although the advantages of AI in our daily lives are undeniable, there are concerns about its dangers. Inadequate physical security, economic losses, and ethical issues are just a few examples of the damage AI could cause. The European Commission has identified examples of unacceptable risk, such as uses of AI that manipulate human behaviour and systems that allow social-credit scoring. For example, the European legal framework would prohibit an AI system that resembles China's social credit scoring. From an intellectual property perspective on AI, the World Intellectual Property Office (WIPO) leads several conversations on Intellectual Property and Frontier Technologies, with the European Union working on a legal framework to regulate artificial intelligence and the UK Intellectual Property Office (UK IPO) leading several consultations on ownership.

1 What Is Artificial Intelligence (AI)?

Marvin Minsky defined AI as intelligent behaviour, saying "AI is the science of making machines do things that would require intelligence if done by men" (Minsky 1961). He omitted to mention women but as the founding figure in AI, we can forgive the omission. This is now considered weak AI as with the speed of developments, there is a demand for stronger AI that not only requires intelligence but identically mirrors human intelligence. David Fogel (2005) went further to identify strong AI as "the study of intelligent behaviour. Its ultimate goal is a theory of intelligence that accounts for the behaviour of naturally occurring intelligent entities and that guides the creation of artificial entities capable of intelligent behaviour".

The three waves of AI were described in a presentation by DARPA's John Launchbury (2017). He set out how artificial intelligence capabilities can be divided into three distinct waves of; handcrafted knowledge (describe), statistical learning (categorise) and contextual adaption (explain). Launchbury's definition of first-wave AI systems are rule-based systems and human engineers define the rules for AI systems to follow. An example is Turbo Tax that tax lawyers or accountants use to convert the complex tax codes into rules, these AI systems do not have learning capability, are poor in handling any uncertainties and can only solve narrowly defined problems. Therefore, it can be said the first wave of AI systems are simply machines following rules that are defined by humans with no substantial difference from electronic tools or equipment that humans use. The second-wave of AI systems have capabilities to define rules through clustering and classifications of massive data – this is significantly different from the first-wave of AI systems and also distinguishable from the third-wave of contextual adaption.

A more recent definition comes from Waymond Rodgers (2020) where he describes three waves of AI, namely narrow, general and super, which builds on the definitions by Launchbury. Narrow AI has only characteristics consistent with cognitive intelligence, it is not conscious, sentient, or driven by emotions the way that individuals are configured to make decisions. General AI represent machines that display human intelligence, that is, they can perform any intellectual task that a human being can in terms of decision-making. Super AI displays features of all kinds of competencies such as emotional and social intelligence, can be self-conscious and self-aware in their interactions with others.

2 Defining Artificial Intelligence Within Intellectual Property Law

AI systems and their advanced development are reshaping the whole creative and innovative sectors that are protected in the existing intellectual property system. Therefore, it is necessary to identify the AI systems at present and to map the direction of AI development in the context of intellectual property law. World Intellectual Property Organisation (WIPO) leads a series of conversations and discussions in AI and intellectual property policy and through the Conversations, WIPO tries to clarify the line between the two concepts: AI- assisted and AI-generated outputs, because they would lead to substantially different recognitions. The division of AI outputs for the purposes of AI can be better seen as three tiers and defined as "AI- supported", "AI-assisted" and "AI-generated".

The least contentious of the three tiers is "AI-supported". This is since the results made by AI-supported systems are predictable by humans. From this perspective, AI-supported outputs are defined as outputs produced by a rule-based computer system that fully follows the rules defined by humans, without the substantial intelligent ability (which embraces learning, perceiving, abstracting and reasoning). In this case, humans are authors/inventors of AI-supported outputs because the outputs are a result of humans' full material intervention and therefore owners of the intellectual property. The AI-support in the creative process is limited to a digital tool for scientists, entrepreneurs and artists, enabling new human inventions and creations (UK IPO 2022).

The second-wave of AI systems, which can be clearly seen as AI- assisted over AI- supported, relies on the advanced improvement of data and computational power as well as better models of algorithms than seen at the AI-supported wave or handcrafted knowledge. The rising big data and internet technology builds up a giant database, which is a perfect machine learning hub. The more data the AI systems can obtain, the wider knowledge AI systems can learn from and therefore the capability to produce more accurate outputs is enhanced. The second pillar of the success of AI systems is computational power, which means computational capacity. Meanwhile, the present AI systems can use those defined models to predict and make decisions by themselves to some extent.

We can reflect on the first two waves of AI, the first of which was handcrafted knowledge, which still has relevance. The second wave, which is very mainstream with AI systems for face and voice recognition, is focussed on statistical learning where we build systems that get trained on data. However, the two waves by themselves are not going to be sufficient or meet the growing market demand for AI systems and what they can do. We see the need to bring them together and that is evident through a third wave of AI technology built around the concept of contextual adaption (Rodgers 2020).

The term "AI-generated outputs" is defined as outputs made by computer systems that have the freedom to do decision-making during the output generation process through integrating the ability to perceive, abstract, explain and reason by themselves, with minimised (if any) human intervention and embracing their own understanding of the real world. Here, we have the contention between intellectual property protection and AI acknowledgment in the intangible asset industry. There are strong arguments that arts and music are inherently human and as such the associated intellectual property rights can only belong to the human creator. There are several issues with this, first of all, there is little incentive for the AI industry to further develop the third wave of the AI systems if it cannot benefit from intellectual property rights protection. To explain this further, the EU Commission stance on the extension of intellectual property rights to AI and the relationship between each individual intellectual property right and AI will be considered.

3 EU Commission and Artificial Intelligence

The European Parliament resolution of 16 February 2017 made recommendations to the Commission on Civil Law Rules on Robotics (EU Commission on Civil Law Rules on Robotics 2015), followed by a resolution of 20 October 2020 on intellectual property rights for the development of artificial intelligence technologies. The EU Commission has proposed the first ever legal framework on AI, which addresses the risks of AI and positions Europe to play a leading role globally (European Commission, 2021). MEPs approved proposals to address long-term opportunities and legal challenges posed by AI in the area of ethics, civil liability and intellectual property. The question is what is an effective intellectual property system that safeguards innovation and creation where AI applications are involved? There are currently no uniform contractual clauses used by all or most AI service providers.

The Commission report states that EU global leadership in AI requires an effective intellectual property system and safeguards for the EU's patent system to protect developers. MEPs specify that AI should not have legal personality, and "inventorship" should be only granted to humans. a test case before the UK courts (as well as before courts and IP offices globally), in the UK – Thaler v Comptroller General of Patents Trade Marks And Designs [2021] EWCA Civ 1374, has confirmed the position under the current law. All judges in the Court of Appeal agreed that an AI machine cannot be an inventor under the 1977 Patents Act. There was a disagreement, however, as to whether a patent application which contained a statement of inventorship to that effect was valid under the Act, with the majority concluding that it was not.

Members stressed that creating a framework for creativity and innovation by encouraging the use of AI technologies by creators should not be at the expense of the interests of human creators or the Unions ethical principles. They considered it essential in this respect to distinguish between AI-assisted human creations and AI-generated creations. They specified that AI should not be endowed with legal personality, which could have negative effects on the motivation of human creators. Members therefore recommended that rights should only be granted to natural or legal persons who have created the work legally and only if the copyright owner has given permission for the use of copyrighted content. The resolution added that AI or related technologies used for the registration procedure to grant IPRs and for the determination of liability for infringements of IPRs cannot be a substitute for human review carried out on a case-by-case basis, in order to ensure the quality and fairness of decisions.

4 So Where Does That Leave Us?

Let's start with patents. WIPO set the minimum compliance standards for all intellectual property rights that all signatory countries must abide by, knows as trade related intellectual property rights (TRIPS). For patent registration and subsequent protection, the rules set out a four-step test:

(1) The invention is new
(2) An invention shall be taken to involve an inventive step if it is not obvious to a person skilled in the art
(3) An invention shall be taken to be capable of industrial application if it can be made in any kind of industry
(4) It does not fall foul of the exclusions and exceptions

All WIPO signatories by in large follow the same four step test, individual countries will differ on what they deem as an exclusion or exception dependent on the Constitution and commonly these fall under morality or public policy. A patent is an official document that confers proprietorship of an invention on the recipient, grant of a patent is preceded by examination of applications by the patenting authority. The fundamental principle behind patents is that the government awards exclusive control over an invention for a fixed number of years to the individual who first discloses the invention within its territory.

In most systems, a patent is granted to an applicant who is first to submit a detailed description of the invention, for example in the UK, the system operates on a first to file model. The TRIPS agreement sought to set international minimum standards in patent protection and at

Article 27 stated the requirements for; novelty, inventiveness, industrial applicability and exclusions. A successful patent application grants the inventor the right to exclude others from utilising the patented invention for a given amount of time, under the TRIPS Agreement, the monopoly right is granted for twenty years. In return, the inventor is under an obligation to describe the invention in detail to give notice to the public. The counterargument to the monopoly right granted to the inventor is that monopoly is against public interest.

5 To DABUS or Not to DABUS

In oral proceedings in December 2021, the Legal Board of Appeal of The European Patent Office (EPO) presided over the case of DABUS and dismissed the appeal in cases J 8/20 and J 9/20.

The Legal Board of Appeal confirmed the decisions of the Receiving Section of the European Patent Office to refuse the applications EP 18 275 163 and EP 18 275 174, to not recognize DABUS, an artificial intelligence system, as the inventor on the patent application. The EPO therefore came to the decision that AI cannot be named as the inventor on patent applications and confirmed previous decisions whereby an inventor in a patent application must be a human being under the European Patent Convention (EPC).

The dismissal of the DABUS case by the EPO Legal Board of Appeal is just one of the appeals brought forward by Stephen Thaler, to give intellectual property ownership rights to an AI system as the inventor on a patent application. This is not Mr. Thaler's only court battle to have DABUS recognized as a patent inventor. He has had simultaneous applications in several countries. For example, in the UK, in September 2021, the Court of Appeal also dismissed the appeal and upheld that the protection afforded to human inventors cannot be extended to AI systems. However, although the UK and EPO are effectively singing off the same IP hymn sheet, Mr. Thaler has been successful in South Africa (Cochrane and Mhangwane 2022). Therefore, the more pressing question raised by the DABUS case is whether the intellectual property laws that have been designed to protect creative human endeavors, can be extended to AI systems.

For patent protection, on the whole, as it currently stands the answer is no. This links back to the focus of this chapter, who should own the intellectual property asset and reap the economic benefits generated by the intellectual effort. There are inherent weaknesses in the intellectual property system and TRIPS in general as there is no clear provision for what an AI system needs to demonstrate to meet the requirements of patent protection. When the distinction between human intellectual effort and AI effort becomes more difficult to define, there will be repeated calls from a whole generation of Mr. (and Mrs) Thalers'. As AI develops through the different cycles of AI assisted and AI generated, the next cycle will be far more sophisticated. It is important to note, that the several consultations carried out by IP offices on the ownership of patent rights by AI systems don't recommend a like for like patent ownership test. There are obvious reasons for this, the speed at which advanced AI systems could meet the current patent test could be much faster than the human inventor and consequently, the duration times for any protection that may be afforded in the future would need to reflect this.

6 The Copyright and AI Battle

Looking at copyright on the other hand, it is evident that the rules are less clear when compared to patents and AI applications, AI is heavily used in the music industry and could impact copyright laws. Questions that need to be considered are what does AI have to offer music producers, and is it a boon or a threat to people who make music for a living? What does it mean for copyright protection?

Turning attention to the UK copyright laws, the Copyright Design Patent Act (CDPA 1988) at section 9(1) defines the '"author", in relation to a work, as the person who creates it, therefore a natural person. Copyright is automatic as established by the idea expression dichotomy from TRIPS article 9(2). The test for copyright is that it must be original and this is a fairly low benchmark. Most importantly, the copyright work must fit into a category and some level of effort, a sufficient level of skill, labour and judgement is required as well as the requirement that it can be fixed.

After several consultations on Copyright and IP, the UK IPO has confirmed that a copyright work can be created by a human who has assistance from AI. If the work expresses original human creativity it will benefit from copyright protection like a work created using any other tool. By default then, if the work is AI assisted or generated and lacks original human creativity, it cannot be classed as a copyright work.

Exclusion apply to computer generated works as a sui generis right. CDPA section 178 a computer generated work with no human author, the "author" of a "computer- generated work" (CGW) is defined as "the person by whom the arrangements necessary for the creation of the work are undertaken". The protection lasts for 50 years from the date the work is made.

Distinction between when there is human involvement to when there isn't needs to be made more clear which can be achieved with a tiered distinction between AI assisted and AI generated in all categories of copyright, not only computer generated works.

The extent and nature of human involvement needs to be specified. Does it suffice if a human instructs an AI application to produce music of a specific genre? Is that sufficient to make the resulting work fall outside the qualification of AI generated work? This is relevant to authorship and ownership of the work. Thinking about the creative process in AI-assisted outputs, who does the creative process in AI-assisted started with, what is the equivalent production for the idea expression dichotomy (Fig. 1).

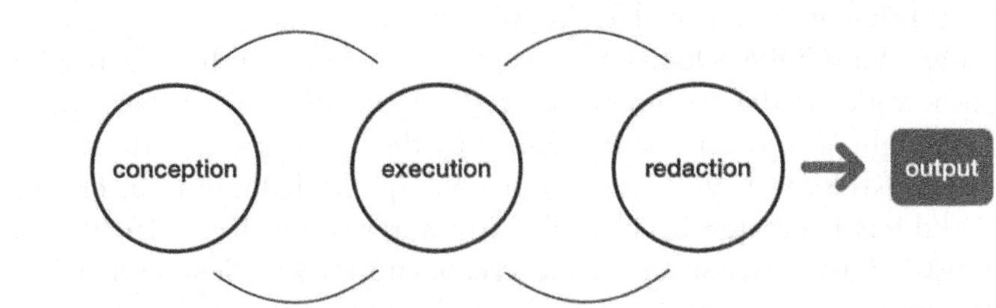

Fig. 1 The idea expression dichotomy

There are several stages identified when assessing AI assistance in copyright works starting with the conception stage. Under AI assisted outputs, this would be the human creator as the designer, working on the specifications, elaborating a work at this stage. Next, there is an execution stage where draft versions are produced and this is where the work is predominantly carried out by the AI system. The final stage of the creative process reverts back to the human creator as redaction require editing and finalising the work. For example, a musician using an AI music composer will often edit the output before releasing the music as a final work. While AI systems play a dominant role at the execution phase, the role of human authors at the conception stage often remains essential.

Moreover, in many instances, human beings will also oversee the redaction stage. Depending on the facts of the case, this will allow human beings sufficient creative choice. Assuming these choices are expressed in the final AI-assisted output, the output will then qualify as a copyright-protected work. By contrast, if an AI system is programmed to automatically execute content without the output being conceived or redacted by a person exercising creative choices, there will be no work, it will be considered AI generated and in the public domain.

The EU Commission report identified a four-step test for the assessment of copyright protection of subject matter as a "work" where AI plays a part. (from the EU Commission IP Action Plan).

The test is:

(1) a "production in the literary, scientific or artistic domain";
(2) the product of human intellectual effort;
(3) originality – the result of creative choices; and
(4) expression – the creative choices "expressed" in the output.

Artificial intelligence in the music industry is a topic of interest, given the level of dependency human music creators place on artificial intelligence systems to support the creation of the musical work. The economic value of music copyright globally is estimated at $40 billion (Cooke 2022) and the role artificial intelligence plays in the creation of copyrightable work, leads to legal and policy implications in this field.

The Institute for Information Law (IViR) and Centre for International Intellectual Property Studies (CEIPI) carried out a survey looking at music and AI outputs and found many of the AI music outputs examined will likely pass steps (1), (2) and (4). The crux of the test is therefore in step (3), the core of the originality standard under copyright law. From this perspective then, where an output does not qualify as original in the sense that it reflects the author's free and creative choices, that output is, from the perspective of copyright, in the public domain. Although it could still benefit from protection under related rights, where is the incentive for artificial system creators to further enhance and improve the offering of systems if the current copyright laws exclude the AI generated work from protection (Bulayenko 2017).

In the context of step (3), it is possible in the first place to identify a series of external constraints on the assessment of originality: rule- based, technical, functional, and informational. The existence of such constraints reduces the author's margin for creative freedom, sometimes below the originality threshold. In the second place, the step allows for the identification of three iterative stages of the creative process when using an AI system: "conception", "execution", and "redaction" as discussed above. The iterative stages could support the qualification of AI outputs for copyright protected work. (Grauwe and Gryspeerdt 2022).

7 Can the Four-Step Test Be Applied to AI-Generated Outputs and Pave the Way for AI Ownership of Copyright?

In the landmark Infopaq case (Infopaq International 2009) heard before the Court of Justice of the European Union (C- 5/08 Infopaq International A/S v Danske Dagbaldes Forening), that Court held that copyright only applies to original works that reflect the author's own intellectual creation as seen in the copyright four step test. The decision upheld the conservative view that a human author is necessary for a copyright work to demonstrate and meet the necessary intellectual creativity requirement.

Despite the requirement for human intellectual creativity, the challenges to copyright laws where artificial intelligence is concerned continues. In 2016, The Rembrandt 2.0 was created as a computer-generated artwork. The pertinent question raised by the Rembrandt 2.0 is on who should own the copyright and is a useful benchmark for the four step AI copyright test. Let's first look at the work itself and how it was generated. The aim of work was not to create a specific painting per se, but rather, to utilise the Artificial Intelligence systems at the disposal of the creative team and create a simulation. An extensive range of expertise were gathered in the creation of the Rembrandt 2.0. ING and the J. Walter Thompson agency in Amsterdam commissioned the project with the use of a computer from Cornell University researchers that had taught itself physics and the Deep Dream Generator from Google for surreal photographs. Algorithms were designed with traditional data analysis systems to create a digital artwork painting that followed the artistic style and creativity of the seventeenth century Dutch artist (Guadamuz 2017).

The goal of ING and the J. Walter Thompson agency was to discover if an algorithm could be created to produce a physical work of art that in essence, would be the nearest effort to a genuine Rembrandt painting. The Rembrandt team, consisting of data scientists, engineers, and art historians analysed over 300 Rembrandt's painting and his techniques, style and subject matter. 150 gigabytes of digitally rendered graphics were collected to provide the instruction set to produce the textures and layers necessary for Rembrandt 2.0 and transfer that knowledge into the software which could generate the new work using the latest in 3D printing technology. Who then should the copyright belong to and are the current copyright laws and frameworks sufficient?

Applying the four-step test to Rembrandt 2.0, for step 1, the work is a digital painting and therefore fits the category of a production in the artistic domain. For step 2, the artwork has to demonstrate that it is a product of human intellectual effort which would be the Rembrandt team of experts and their effort and step 4 is met by the expression of the output. Focussing then on step 3, we know AI can support the creative process provided the originality test is met by a human, copyright law has yet to develop a test that distinguishes between when the AI is a tool in the creative process or actually the decision maker that meets the originality test.

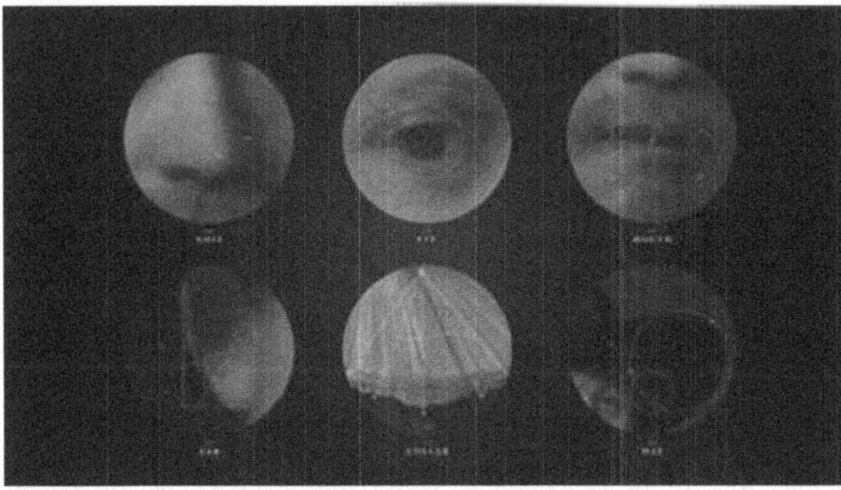

J. Walter Thompson Amsterdam (2016)

8 Non-human Actors in the Originality Test

To have AI as a non-human actor in the originality test has both advantages and disadvantages. The clear disadvantage is that the rule is too broad brushed, essentially placing AI systems and monkeys in the same category. In the Compendium of US Copyright Practices § 313.2, the section clearly states what cannot be registered for copyright protection and includes a photograph taken by a monkey as well as a machine. For one, the monkey selfie was a rare and complete stroke of luck photograph, the monkey could not satisfy the test for copyright protection and therefore the US Court correctly held that the image could not belong to the monkey.

On the US Copyright Practices on machines, the section states:

> The Office will not register works produced by a machine or mere mechanical process that operates randomly or automatically without any creative

input or intervention from a human author. The crucial question is "whether the 'work' is basically one of human authorship, with the computer [or other device] merely being an assisting instrument, or whether the traditional elements of authorship in the work (literary, artistic, or musical expression or elements of selection, arrangement, etc.) were actually conceived and executed not by man but by a machine. (U.S. Copyright Office 1966).

This links back to the initial argument of this chapter as to whether the current divide between AI assisted and AI generated requires further clarification or better yet, whether a third wave of AI will address step 3 of the copyright test and be able to fulfil all three iterative stages of the originality test.

9 Artificial Intelligence: A Black Swan for Intellectual Property Systems?

Intellectual property (IP) law was treated as a law stimulating creation and innovation through rewarding human creative and innovative activities so as to encourage continuing investment in creation and innovation. Artificial intelligence (AI), being a frontier technology, is challenging the existing IP framework and testing boundaries of fundamentals of IP systems. First of all, AI engages creativity and innovation that were treated as human-only areas. Therefore, there is a debate on whether AI and its outputs should be protected, can be protected, and how to treat these issues via existing IP context. Furthermore, the concept of stimulating creation and innovation through a rewarding system is not suitable for AI as machines would actively produce creative/innovative outputs without any rewarding purpose. In this case, it is worthy to understand whether the existing IP system would stimulate AI- related innovation and investment and what kind of legal system is able to offer such effort in a wider legal context. The focus now will be to analyse the AI challenges that IP systems face and explore how the law might respond to these challenges in the purpose of stimulating AI investment and development. For there to be another wave of AI, that is beyond a contextual adaption of the

AI-assisted and AI-generated waves, there needs to be an IP system in place that recognises the AI input, otherwise apart from the contractual benefits for producing more sophisticated AI, there is little reward from an IP perspective.

There is considerable economic investment that goes into the development of AI systems and if there are no IP laws to protect the work that is created, it must then be free to use in the public domain. Therefore, despite AI being the black swan of intellectual property systems, it needs it's own set of IP laws that are specifically tailored to AI related IP.

In the next wave of research in the relationship between IP and AI systems, the developments made by AI systems will require a stage of "contextual adaptation" according to Launchbury (2017).

To better support the recognition of the work created by AI systems in this stage and further the conversation on IP protection for AI works, this would necessitate the AI system understand and perceive the real world by themselves and no longer be reliant on massive data but learn more from an understanding of the real-world phenomena and reason with it. There are ambitions to create a wave of AI which allows machines and humans to communicate more naturally. Launchbury further states that the next wave of AI systems could create AI learning with the ability to perceive complex and subtle information, conceive and learn within an environment, execute the learning to create new meanings and exercise a redaction process to make final decisions. The stumbling block for the current wave of AI systems is an inability to satisfy step 3 of the copyright test.

With the next wave AI system, there is scope to reduce the need for human intervention and to further expand the ability of the AI system from a highly efficient tool to an AI system that can create new IP assets using its own reasoning and equivalent thinking mind.

This is akin to the future success of AI systems that can not only start thinking independently, but they are also capable of making internal linkages within their digital environment, apply reasoning and deduction skills to satisfy the human test component of intellectual property ownership and resultingly, have an argument to benefit from the economic protection that IP affords human owners. The door on IP protection in broader areas for AI, other than computer generated works, is not permanently closed. Rather, as the next wave of AI develops to mimic the human mind and satisfy the tests in place for the different types of IP assets, then it could open a door for AI systems to explore novel intellectual property asset ownership and spearhead the creation of an AI/IP protection system.

10 Legal and Ethical Considerations

Ethical discourse is commonly not a priority in a conventional study of intellectual property and business. Moral sentiments often take a back seat to market sentiments, even in shaping the direction of ethical business strategy (Hoppe 2022). This anomaly persists despite growing interest in ethics and IP. Taking an interdisciplinary and diverse perspective, this section enriches the evolving definition and scope of ethical discourse literature by focusing on intellectual property assets and regulation that shape the business sector.

Considering the gap between theory and practice, and pertinent to the legal and ethical considerations of a future AI/IP protection system, bridging academic knowledge in unpacking ethical and governance issues in the intellectual property industry.

11 Trustworthy AI

Although the advantages of AI in our daily lives are undeniable, there are concerns about its dangers. Inadequate physical security, economic losses, and ethical issues are just a few examples of the damage AI could cause. As discussed earlier, the European Commission has identified examples of unacceptable risk as uses of AI that manipulate human behavior and systems that allow social-credit scoring (European Commission, 2021). For example, the European legal framework would prohibit an AI system similar to China's social credit scoring (Marcia 2021). A legal framework would require minimum level of uniformity at an international level, for example, through the TRIPS agreement or a supplementary provision with staggered grace periods dependent upon individual states' socio-political conditions. Notwithstanding the need for specific criteria, technical knowledge, certifications and implementation procedures (Margoni 2022). The certifications are important as there needs to be an independent governmental and international control mechanism on professional standards for trustworthy AI.

12 Patent Offices and AI

One of the main areas where Patent Offices are considering the use of AI is on how the role of AI in patent offices will be affected by the rapidly developing frontier technologies underpinning the fourth industrial revolution. IP Australia is developing a Trade Mark International Classification Services (TMICS) to support customers with searching the Madrid Goods and Service (MGS) database. Leveraging Natural Language Processing (NLP) models (sentence-transformers), TMICS assists with finding goods and services that match search terms and are also semantically related. The aim is to significantly decrease the number of queries and make the application process more efficient. It saves time for the customers when they are searching through classifications for the relevant goods and services, saving on effort and making the system more user friendly. The attraction of using AI in IP offices is to aid the patent offices in improving the quality of applications. This is also relevant to making applications overseas and is one of the many AI initiatives that IP offices are considering implementing (WIPO, 2018).

The UK IPO recently launched a consultation on potential legislative changes for IPO digital transformation. Similar consultations are taking place in the European Patent Office, the US Patent and Trademark Office and national Patent Offices, to better understand AI-focused transformations to the IP protection and ownership process (Barazza 2021). The UK IPO consultation concerned legal policy and regulatory frameworks, to provide clearer guidelines and supporting mechanisms to address flaws and gaps in the existing legal framework. The consultations are addressing the need to move away from paper processes and step into a digitally-led era. The law was designed for a paper filing system and any proposed changes to the law need to adapt to enable digital transformation of services (UK IPO Consultation, 2023). Legislation could be altered to better support innovation however this raises concerns over technical expertise, risk management and robust monitoring of the legislative powers especially when delegated.

A preferred legislative approach is crucial to the success of the digital transformation of patent offices as this will allow the patent office to overhaul existing processes and provide a single, integrated digital system to allow for a more efficient system for the registration of IP assets based on whether it is a patent right, trademark or a registered design. As well as building new digital services, governments need to ensure there are legal framework that can support them. This requires flexibility to legally adapt to new technologies, and to respond efficiently to then implement the changes successfully. The economics of AI and AI-generated innovation in IP is still in its infancy, the potential impact of international regulation and how to resolve inconsistencies between varying approach taken by other countries to the same regulatory issues, are part of the reasoning behind giving more legislative powers to the IP offices. The complexities arise when accounting for the rule of law and the lack of precedent for AI friendly IP law.

13 AI in Copyright Law

Starting with the classification of AI in copyright law, both from a theoretical and AI governance point of view, there are a number of issues. In the UK, copyright protection for computer generated works, without a human author, exists and offers fifty years of protection (CDPA 1988). To extend copyright protection beyond computer generated works, an assessment of the current protection is valuable. In the UK IPO's 2022 consultation, the copyright law for computer-generated works was found to be effective, the AI had not been harmful and there had been no significant change in the capacity level of AI systems to warrant further protection, likewise, there was no marked negative impact to justify reversing the current law.

Despite the many attractions of AI led IP law, most notably, for its perceived economic benefits and ability to streamline current processes and methods, the legislative changes require unbiased and independent review. If there is to be a copyright protection system for AI, is it the AI systems that self-regulate or is it the government through IP offices. AI systems are built primarily by software designers and developers who are not required to complete AI related professional ethics training. Thus, a framework for AI Copyright law, which addresses the next wave of AI and how it could meet copyright standards, also needs to deal with AI regulation standards.

AI risks can be positioned against long-established responsible legal principles of intention and culpability in civil and criminal law. AI systems lack capacity for subjective knowledge and intent, therefore proving intent will require a new set of legal rules that set out the parameters for establishing intent. (Yeung 2020). AI certification which evidences the training of the software developer in core areas of ethics, intent, culpability and negligence, would mitigate the risks posed by broadening AI copyright law beyond computer generated works. An examination of Public Law and the impact of AI on the general public, on future human creators will need to be established as part of the overall framework to ensure the AI is trustworthy and where, despite the infrastructure, it is found not to be, requisite remedial protocols are in place.

For copyright law itself, approaching the place that AI has at the copyright dinner table is premature and ill-fitted. Even if the next wave or subsequent waves of AI satisfy the copyright test, it is still a copyright test for humans. Rather than shoehorn AI into a test that was never intended for non-humans, an alternative test could be designed for AI that could potentially grant copyright protection and remedies to the AI system, both individually and jointly with a human. The duration periods will require careful examination to reflect the speed at which AI can create and whether, at least for the first cycle of AI protected copyright law, there is a human check element. For text and data mining, the UK IPO plan to introduce a new copyright and database exception which allows text and data mining for any purpose. There will be safeguarding and mechanisms to protect content, including a requirement for lawful access (UK IPO Consultation, 2022).

14 AI in Patent Law

AI inventions and the possibility of patent ownership remains under review at WIPO, the EU IPO, from the US and the UK. For AI-devised inventions, although the UK IPO will review the legal provisions periodically, there is no change to UK patent law at the moment. Despite the controversial Thaler case and the diverging views on the future of AI based inventions, as discussed earlier, AI is not yet advanced enough to invent without human intervention.

However, as can be seen from the speed at which AI is developing, the margin between what AI can and cannot do without human intervention, continues to shrink. The patent system supports AI innovation and the use of AI as a tool in AI-assisted inventions, enabling human led or at least involved inventions. Changing national laws will always prove to be problematic as if there isn't an international consensus on changing patent laws to give AI inventor rights, the level of protection is territorial and minimal, especially if economic losses need to be recuperated. Contractual clauses that can value the role of the AI system is an interim remedy to recognise the full economic value of AI in patents until there is more development in the AI systems to facilitate inventions without human intervention at any stage.

15 Alas, Who Should the Intellectual Property Belong To?

AI systems have developed rapidly and have been defined as AI-assisted and AI-generated, and AI-assisted can be divided further into an earlier and more premature stage of AI-supported. For AI-supported, it is the first-wave of AI systems, embedded in rule-based programming with human creators defining very specific and clear rules for AI systems to follow, with little room for AI creativity. Turbo Tax falls within AI-assisted as the AI systems do not have learning capability, nor are the systems equipped to handle uncertainties and can only solve narrowly defined problems.

Therefore, AI-supported systems are predictable by humans and there is no innovation or creativity in the outcomes produced. Essentially, AI-supported outputs are what the wave sys on the tin, they support the production of an output by following rule-based programming defined by humans, without demonstrating the components of intelligent ability. AI-supported systems are devoid of the core human intelligent skills, such as, learning, perceiving, abstracting and reasoning. It is clear that the human engineers are the authors of AI-supported outputs and under the legal rules of intellectual property, the rightful owners of the intellectual property assets.

Where the conversation on intellectual property ownership gains traction is when considering the definitions of AI-assisted and AI-generated. As a summary, the current law on this is clear. AI-assistance in the generation of IP assets is seen as a supportive tool in assisting the human creators and inventors. However, as highlighted in this chapter, and further in subsequent chapters, the distinction between when there is human involvement to when there isn't needs to be reassessed and refined. The clearer the distinction between AI assisted and AI generated, the more incentive there is for AI systems to evolve to the next wave and meet the current international IP standards. The extent and nature of human involvement needs to be specified. If the AI-assistance is taking a lead in the final production of the IP asset, the parameters of what is a minimum level of human involvement also requires more transparency and clarity. For AI-generated, the UK and other nations have exemptions in place, as can be seen from the discussion of computer-generated works.

From preliminary analysis of the DABUS case and the Rembrandt 2.0, the current legal provisions on IP protection have a short life expectancy as there is strong evidence that AI systems are becoming more sophisticated and the next wave of AI could see AI-generated outputs that fall outside the scope of computer-generated works. The DABUS case is further examined throughout the remaining chapters with diverging views on its application and importance to patent law. The closer analysis of patent and copyright law does support the existing EU Commission views and the results of several consultations in the UK on whether AI should have ownership rights in intellectual property law. In conclusion, it is still too early to develop an IP system that has minimum level of standards for AI. The reasoning for this is that the AI systems, albeit far more sophisticated in the current wave of AI, still lack sentient ability and despite the ability for AI to create a product, the role of a human is still required. However, there will be a further wave of AI, and the exception of computer-generated works will not suffice to meet the intellectual effort of AI. The next stage for intellectual property law policy and ethics is to create the framework where AI and humans can both have an equitable slice of the IP pie.

References

Barazza, S. The Year Of Data?, Journal of Intellectual Property Law & Practice, Volume 16, Issue 2, February 2021, Pages 89–90, https://doi.org/10.1093/jiplp/jpab024

Bulayenko, O, Frosio, G and Geiger, C. Opinion of the CEIPI on the European Commission's Proposal to Reform Copyright Limitations and Exceptions in the European Union, Centre for International Intellectual Property Studies (CEIPI) Research Paper No. 2017–09.

Cochrane, D and Mhangwane, C. Dabus: rise of inventive machines, (2022). Spoor and Fisher. Available at https://spoor.com/dabus-the-rise-of-the-inventive-machines/.

Cooke, C. Will Page says "music copyright has never had it so good" as global revenues reach almost $40 billion (2022), Complete Music Update.

Copyright, Design and Patent Act 1988

EU Commission on Civil Law Rules on Robotics (2015/2103(INL)

European Commission, Coordinated Plan On Artificial Intelligence 2021 Review. Available at https://digital-strategy.ec.europa.eu/en/library/coordinated-plan-artificial-intelligence-2021-review

Fogel, D. Evolutionary Computation: Toward a New Philosophy of Machine Intelligence, Third Edition, (2005), Wiley.

Grauwe, D P and Gryspeerdt, S. Artificial intelligence (AI): The qualification of AI creations as "works" under EU copyright law, (2022), Grewer.

Guadamuz, A. Artificial intelligence and copyright (2017) World Intellectual Property Office Magazine.

Hoppe, M. Theories and Applications of Artificial Intelligence. (2022). United Kingdom: States Academic Press.

Infopaq International A/S v Danske Dagblades Forening (C-5/08) EU:C:2009:465 (16 July 2009).

Launchbury, J. 'DARPA Perspective on AI' (Defense Advanced Research Projects Agency) 2017. https://www.darpa.mil/about-us/darpa-perspective-on-ai

Li, L. Intervention Report for the WIPO Conversation on Intellectual Property and Artificial Intelligence (Third Session) (2020) WIPO https://www.wipo.int/export/sites/www/about-ip/en/artificial_intelligence/conversation_ip_ai/pdf/ind_li.pdf

Minsky, M. Steps Toward Artificial Intelligence in Proceedings of the IRE, Vol. 49, No. 1, 1961, pp. 8–30

Marcia, V. The EU path towards regulation on artificial intelligence, Techtank, 2021.

Margoni, T. A Deeper Look into the EU Text and Data Mining Exceptions: Harmonisation, Data Ownership, and the Future of Technology, GRUR International, 71(8), 2022, 685–701.

Rodgers, W. Artificial Intelligence in a Throughput Model: Some Major Algorithms (Routledge 2020)

Thaler v Comptroller General of Patents Trade Marks And Designs [2021] EWCA Civ 1374 UK Intellectual Property Office Consultations and Publications

U.S. Copyright Office, Report To The Librarian Of Congress By The Register Of Copyrights, 1966

Walter Thompson Amsterdam, 2016 World Intellectual Property Office

Yeung, K. Response to European Commission White Paper on Artificial Intelligence. 2020.

Fostering Innovation by Utilising Big Data: The Data Act and the Risk of Quasi-Exclusivity Reinforcing Data Lockups

Marc A. Stuhldreier

1 Introduction

In *Thaler v Commissioner of Patents* [2021] *FCA 879*, a judge of the Federal Court of Australia for the first time found that an artificial intelligence (AI) can satisfy the requirements to be regarded as an inventor according to Australian patent laws. While the judgement was revoked in 2022, and other courts around the world do not seem to follow the initial court's approach anytime soon, this case provides an indication of how AI and the Big Data which feeds its learning processes slowly but steadily tend to pick up a 'life' of their own. Smart devices, as part of the Internet of Things (IoT), that utilise AI have become prevalent in almost any aspect of our day to day lives, including smart homes, the agricultural sector, and medicinal products. The development, appropriate use and

The original version of this chapter was previously published non-open access. A Correction to this chapter is available at https://doi.org/10.1007/978-3-031-42576-9_9

M. A. Stuhldreier (✉)
Linköping University, Linköping, Sweden
e-mail: marc.stuhldreier@liu.se

N. Naim (ed.), *Developments in Intellectual Property Strategy*,
https://doi.org/10.1007/978-3-031-42576-9_2

advancement of such smart technologies requires vast amounts of data, commonly referred to as Big Data. Thus, the collecting and processing of such data becomes increasingly important to modern life, and the contemporary smart way of living. The mining of such data constitutes an essential requirement for the smart technologies business sector and is pivotal for its future.

This requirement is starkly contrasted, however, by the rights of those who generate the data. Users of smart technologies become workers for the creation of value to industry, even in their leisure-time, irrespective of their awareness of this fact (Noto La Diega 2022a). Notably, the generated user-data may regularly be of a personal nature wherefore this way of collecting data constitutes much more than simple work. Further, questions arise as to the ownership of user generated data which currently is under the factual control of the data holder, with users having few opportunities to access and utilise this data themselves. This leads to a problem of so-called data enclosures or data lock-ins, by which data holders retain the power over the user generated data and lock this data away, preventing not only the re-use of this data by the users, but also hinder access to such data for innovative purposes. Considering the legal and ethical questions concerning the generation and utilisation of this type of data, the traditional legal distinction between online-offline issues is not sufficient to deal with the intricacies of big data, AI, and smart technologies (Noto La Diega 2022a). Various specialised laws and regulations were thus introduced, regulating specific issues in specific fields. Adding to this wide array of regulations, on 23 February 2022 the EU Commission proposed the Regulation on Harmonised Rules on Fair Access to and Use of Data (Data Act) which was formally endorsed by the European Parliament on 9 November 2023 and adopted by the Council on 15 November 2023. As a key pillar of Europe's strategy for dealing with data, the Data Act shall become an important contribution to adequately facilitating digital transformation. The main scope of the Data Act regulates the conditions under which and by whom value can be created from data. To this end, the Data Act adopts specific objectives, including (1) setting up of rules for the utilisation of user-generated data as to ensure fairness in its use, (2) establishing consistency relating to data access rights, which under current (non-)regulation may vary distinctly, and (3) increasing the amount of available data, benefiting companies, citizens, and public administrations alike. In addition to these main objectives, the EU recognises the need of facilitating access to data for the purpose of fostering innovation with societal objectives, and for responding to current challenges including in the fields of public health, agriculture and for achieving the Sustainable Development Goals (SDGs). With its 50 Articles, the Data Act thus sets ambitious goals as to creating a level playing field for the various stakeholders in what may be called user-generated data. The task of striking an adequate balance is complicated by the number of contrasting interests at stake. Concerns can be raised over questions of access to data, its ownership, the protection of personality rights of the users that provide the data, and particularly their right to self-determination. On the other hand, increasing access to user-generated data calls into question the protection of the legitimate rights of the inventors of smart technologies. Ultimately, while recent EU legislation aims for opening data lockups to make data accessible and re-usable, the scope of these regulations seems to in fact strengthen the position of data holders, providing them with further legal measures to maintain their data enclosures (Noto La Diega 2022b).

In this respect, this contribution scrutinises the provisions of the Data Act to analyse *whether the Data Act is successful in striking an adequate balance between the rights and obligations of the various stakeholders in user-generated big data.* Further, this chapter seeks to ascertain *whether the Data Act provides for sufficient accessibility to facilitate that data can be re-used for innovation activity toward societal objectives.*

2 Utilising the Value of Big Data: Innovation in the Fourth Industrial Revolution (4IR)

2.1 Big Data

In the digital age, data can be loosely described as a unit containing digital information. While information was always a valuable asset to humanity and thus sensitive for businesses, states and citizens, data can now be defined as a building block in the modern digital economy (Burri 2021;

Irion 2021). This digital economy can also be described as data-driven in that it is "built around the collection, preservation, protection, implementation and understanding of many different types of data." (Aaronson 2021). The McKinsey Global Institute suggested in a 2016 report that the global economy has now entered an era that is 'defined by data flows' (Manyyika et al. 2016). Indeed, in today's economy, data, or better big data, has introduced a new era in global trade, in which data has transitioned into becoming a commodity in itself (Gervais 2021).

Big data refers to the amassing and storing of extensive and exponentially growing data sets. While there is no single generally valid definition, big data is often defined as datasets exhibiting three essential features, a fourth additional feature and a derivative fifth feature. These features can be conceptualised as the five V's; high volume, veracity, velocity, variety, and value. Volume refers to the size of data sets or simply the sheer amount of data generated. Veracity of automatically collected data refers to data quality and its trustworthiness. Velocity concerns the pace at which data is generated, while variety refers to the different data types and its numerous sources. Lastly, value refers to the current or future value of these datasets, for corporations and other stakeholders with regard to their utilisation for economic, innovative, or societal objectives (Burri 2021; Gervais 2021). In addition, big data can be generally categorised as either structured or unstructured. Structured data is data that is sufficiently clear to be utilised for a purpose, while unstructured data, which may include meta data collected as a side-product of using a digital device or different types of free texts in online forms, generally requires further structuring before its value can be unlocked (Jülicher 2018).

Today, exponential amounts of data are generated by machines and human activity in the digital society, where smart devices and smart infrastructure, including smart homes, smart health, and smart cities, are readily available and frequently used in modern life (Irion 2021; Storr and Storr 2017). In fact, data-collection opportunities arise in most aspects of modern life where almost everything is connected by data-driven technologies and mobile internet (Aaronson 2021). In the sphere of the Internet of things (IoT), the success of wearable technologies, or wearables, exemplifies how data can be collected and to a certain extent analysed in real time when valuable health information is gathered by fitness trackers and successively processed in their connected apps. While the large amounts of data generated by wearables can be utilised for the user's and society's benefit, the risk of this data being abused for creating user profiles, providing unwanted insights into their personal sphere rises simultaneously. This is particularly concerning when considering that users of smart technologies predominantly lack the knowledge to understand how their data is processed and utilised (Jülicher and Delisle 2018).

Notably, as types of body-attached computers, wearables not only come in the form of fitness trackers, but also as smartwatches and smart glasses which generate enormous amounts of user specific data, covering most aspects of day-to-day life. Innovative wearable technologies are frequently developed with researchers working, among others, on smart contact lenses, smart tattoos, and smart fashion, such as intelligent socks, providing further opportunities for the production and analysis of expansive datasets (Jülicher and Delisle 2018; Storr and Storr 2017). This digitalisation of society and the economy, which is now also regarded as the fourth industrial revolution (4IR), leads to a growing fusion of different technologies, "rewriting the boundaries between biological, physical, and digital." (Noto La Diega and Derclaye 2023).

The utilisation of big data is generally based on linking the data that was collected from different devices and other sources. Oftentimes, data is initially collected without a specific purpose and stored until it may become useful at a later time. Linking in the big data context is thus not only concerned with combining data that was collected from different sources but also with combining new data and existing prior generated data. Considering that a large amount of such data is generated by users through their use of personal smart devices, these datasets often contain personal data, which, according to the purpose limitation principle of the General Data Protection Regulation (GDPR), can legally only be collected for specific purposes (Culik 2018). While not all user generated data necessarily is of personal nature, big data and the mode of its collection often blur the lines between personal and non-personal. In fact, user generated data can rarely be fully anonymised (Burri 2021).

To derive value from big data, and particularly for unlocking the potential of unstructured data, relevant information needs to be extracted from large datasets and organised. Such activities are commonly referred to as data mining. Notably, data mining can be conducted for purposes that differ from the purposes for which the data was initially collected (Jülicher 2018). As a manual evaluation of the sheer amount of data collected in big datasets is virtually impossible, the mining of data is conducted by utilising AI algorithms that facilitate machine learning processes, enabling the machines to create high value outputs and gain new insights from the raw data (Gervais 2021; Jülicher 2018). These insights then not only reflect the past, but can actively be utilised to predict future trends (Jülicher 2018).

2.2 The Importance of Big Data for Future Innovation in the 4IR

The importance of big data for the digital economy lies in its potential value not just for the original data collector, but for a variety of stakeholders (Jülicher 2018). Additional stakeholders include the users of smart technology as well as, for example, manufacturers, aftermarket service providers, insurances, health service providers, and public and private sector researchers (Jülicher and Delisle 2018). Fully unlocking the potential of big data can provide enterprises with previously unknown information. New insights derived through data analytics, such as identified patterns and conclusions that indicate future trends, are big data's predominant economic value, helping businesses to improve their decisions and strategies (Storr and Storr 2017; Seuba 2021). Unsurprisingly, big data is now of enormous economic interest, both for its value as a business asset as well as for its future value that can be derived by unlocking its innovative potential. In this regard, big data, and particularly personal data, is often referred to as the new oil (Storr and Storr 2017). By not only facilitating more efficient business operations but by also fostering better innovation big data has vast potential to positively serve the public interest (Burri 2021).

It is recognised today that data is key to achieving sustainability and that adequately unlocking its potential is of enormous value for the common good. Access to and utilisation of data, for example, are considered to be a key factor in achieving climate justice and sustainable innovation

(Noto La Diega and Derclaye 2023). Similarly, health data collected from wearables can be utilised to improve personal health by amending personal habits before health conditions occur, thereby helping to mitigate modern public health issues (Storr and Storr, 2017). To make adequate use of the information contained in big datasets, and to achieve these societal objectives, it is crucial to unlock the potential of the collected data. To be effective, it is important to recognise that data mining can be conducted to gain new insights from currently unused big data, not only by the data collector but by other stakeholders with access to the data as well. For this to be effective at large, however, open access to the locked-up data would be required. While competitors on the markets and the general public thus have both economic and public interests in gaining access to and utilising available data, the collectors of big data and those who analyse it tend to also seek (legal) protection for their respective interests in the data and its value (Gervais 2021). Overly strong protection, either via legal instruments such as intellectual property (IP) laws, or through the factual control exercised by the data holder, can in turn lockup data, hamper its utilisation, and prevent the realisation of big data's full potential for the societal benefit.

2.3 Unlocking the Value/Potential of Big Data

One of the main concerns is that currently a relatively small number of companies dominate the global digital economy and thereby exercise a quasi-control of the digital markets, both in developed markets as well as in the developing world (Gervais 2021). This control of the digital economy was facilitated by a modern phenomenon termed 'digital dispossession' by which data collectors amass vast amounts of personal and non-personal data through appropriation. Digital dispossession further provides data holders with a new type of 'data power' which facilitates further data lockups with detrimental impacts on both innovation and aftermarket services (Noto La Diega and Derclaye 2023). When considering the importance of data in modern power dynamics, questions arise as to how data can be utilised appropriately, how data ownership should be regulated, how access can be facilitated, and how incentives can be maintained for investments into the generation of new data.

2.3.1 Data Ownership

As a baseline, it can be emphasized that Data is frequently generated by human action, with machines being merely used for its processing (Noto La Diega and Derclaye 2023). Concerning the ownership of user generated data, it is relatively straight forward to suggest that actual content created by a user, such as email texts, are clearly the ownership of the user. Similarly, photographs taken by a user with the camera of a connected devices fall within the IP of that user, the author of that image. However, the situation may be less clear with further data that is collected through the camera, via sensors or through user input in devices (Storr and Storr 2017). In general, users tend to lack having any influence regarding the use and evaluation of such data (Jülicher and Delisle 2018). Particularly when personal data is processed, technology allows the collectors or holders of user generated data to create user profiles supplemented with information about location, habits, interests, political views or the sexuality of the users (Röttgen 2018, von Schönfeld and Wehkamp 2018). If appropriated, email texts, for example, can be analysed for key words and facilitate further profiling opportunities with economic benefits for the data collector (Röttgen 2018). The prevalent power asymmetries between data collectors and technology users generally leave the users with almost no individual control over the processing of their data (Thouvenin and Tamò-Larrieux 2021).

Narrowing down the perspective, there exist two main issues concerning the ownership of data that need to be balanced: (1) the rights of users, including the protection of their privacy in relation to personal data, and (2) the rights of data holders with respect to investment protection and intellectual property. The concept of data ownership can then be understood two-fold as a property right in data, either directly introduced by law or indirect through a position of factual control which is protected by law (Thouvenin and Tamò- Larrieux 2021). It is to note that currently there exists no IP right or similar property right for data (yet) (Storr and Storr 2017; Podszun and Pfeifer 2022). Without such a right, and in consideration of the enormous interest in data by a variety of stakeholders, questions arise as to who should be the owner of the data, or whose interests take precedent (Storr and Storr 2017). In reality, while there is no general legal property right to data, data holders can rely on other measures such as trade secret protection and database rights as well as technical and contractual measures to effectively establish a property-like protection, providing them with a technical-factual position of data ownership (Noto la Diega 2023; Podszun and Pfeifer 2022; Storr and Storr 2017). Additionally, in the EU, the creator of a databank can own the data contained in this databank via a *sui generis* right established by the EU Database Directive (96/9/EC).

The main concern with property and property-like rights is that historically, property rights derived from the need to regulate scarce resources. Data, however, is not scarce and its use by one party does not exclude another party from extracting value from the same data (Storr and Storr 2017; Hornung and Schomberg 2022). This general non-scarcity of data is also where its main potential lies if data is made sufficiently accessible (Hornung and Schomberg 2022). With various technical difficulties already hampering the adequate sharing of data, a property-like right in data, adding a further layer of complications, can severely exacerbate problems concerning the accessibility and utilisation of data by the various stakeholders. Ultimately, property rights tend to be of an exclusive nature, meaning that non-right holders, including the general society the very users who generate the data, can be excluded from enjoying the benefits arising from big data (Storr and Storr 2017).

While this recognition provides a strong argument against a property right to data, a balanced approach to the question of ownership also needs to take account of concomitant questions and debates concerning the protection of investments and the maintaining of incentives for the future generation of data. In essence, similar to the debates on industrial IP rights, the incentive argument suggests that investors in data generating products and services need to be incentivised to make such investments by receiving protection which prevents competitors who did not make similar investments from using the generated data (Kerber 2022). Conversely, it may be argued that such incentives are less relevant in the context of big data, particularly when collected via IoT devices, as the data collection occurs automatically as a by-product of the regular use of such devices. Thus, the required investment into the data collection itself is marginal, and the development of the IoT devices is likely to be already protected by conventional IP rights (Storr and Storr 2017). Additionally, the value of the data itself, even if simultaneously used by other stakeholders, may provide a sufficient incentive for companies to invest into its collection. As recognised by the EU Data Act, the situation may be different for small and medium sized enterprises (SMEs), who may in fact face substantial investments to set up a data collection business. New start-ups could thus potentially be disincentivised if their collected data would be open to everyone (SWD(2022) 34 final Annex 8).

All things considered, however, and with particular regard to the vast amounts of data that are continuously collected, it seems unsuitable to suggest that further legal incentives for the collection of data are required (Noto La Diega and Derclaye 2023). In this respect, the Max Planck Institute for Innovation and Competition concluded in 2016 that there is neither a requirement nor a justification for introducing a legal exclusive right to data (Drexl et al. 2016). Quite the opposite, it seems that new incentives are actually required to open up data as data holding enterprises oftentimes refrain from voluntarily sharing and facilitating the utilisation of their data for innovation by others (Noto La Diega and Derclaye 2023).

The discussion so far focussed on the concept of ownership for data collectors. From a different perspective, data ownership, or a property right to data could be granted to the users of connected devices, who, through their use, create the data in the first place. It is questionable, however, whether such a property right of the user would be fruitful, or whether it would, in fact, harm the interests of users. While on the surface, a property right would provide the user with the power over their data, a property right can also be traded away, with potential detrimental impacts on the user's privacy. Once sold, the data property to personal data could be owned by corporations, which would potentially negate the positive protection impacts of privacy laws, such as the GDPR (Storr and Storr 2017; Thouvenin and Tamò-Larrieux 2021). One of the concomitant risks is that the buyer of a user's (personal) data could successively exclude the user from accessing and using their own personal data (Thouvenin and Tamò-Larrieux 2021). However, at least with regard to the right to erasure, the GDPR seems to override any other agreements made between the individual and other (economic) actors. It thus seems that, compared to an ownership right in user generated non-personal data, privacy rights are stronger in that they cannot generally be traded away (Storr and Storr 2017). In theory, data ownership could thus potentially help mitigating some of the prevailing problems of the digital economy by providing individuals with a better negotiation position vis-à-vis other economic actors (Thouvenin and Tamò-Larrieux 2021). Then again, due to prevalent information asymmetries, it would be easy for corporations to gain ownership of the data, for example, through hidden contractual terms, a problem that already can be observed in the field of data privacy where the use of intransparent consent tick boxes is commonplace.

Ultimately, as long as clear regulations on data ownership and access rights are missing, data collectors and developers of connected devices can implement technical designs for products that provide them with the de-facto control over the data collected by their devices, which then enables them to effectively exclude competition and to prevent other enterprises and organisations from using the available data for innovative activities (Kerber 2022).

2.3.2 A Right to Access

In addition to questions of data ownership, the second big issue for data governance in the digital economy concerns the accessibility and re-use of data. As of yet, there are no general data access rights, neither for businesses vis-à-vis other businesses, nor for government vis-à-vis businesses (Thouvenin and Tamò-Larrieux 2021). The situation, however, is about to change, with the implementation of the European Data Strategy, inter alia, via the EU Data Governance Act, already providing for the accessibility of publicly held data for further utilisation and re-use, and other regulations, including the Data Act, following in the near future. From a business perspective, data is generally viewed as a valuable asset that should not be freely shared, particularly with competitors (Thouvenin and Tamò-Larrieux 2021). Access to data, however, is a precondition for market entry, participation in a supply chain and innovation (SWD(2022)

34 final at 11). Demands of fairness, free competition, and the facilitation of innovativeness thus all require the establishment of better data accessibility (Podszun and Pfeifer 2022).

Quasi-exclusive rights to data, protecting investments, on the other hand, are liable to abuse and can be utilised to restrict competition with negative impacts on market growth and innovation, further hindering technological development (Storr and Storr 2017). As a result, restrictions of the accessibility of data are likely to have adverse impacts on the digital economy at large (Thouvenin and Tamò-Larrieux 2021). In fact, even before the age of digital data, barriers to the free flow of information were considered detrimental to economic and innovative activity (Burri 2021). If regarded as a public good, the full potential of data could be realised through its utilisation by a variety of stakeholders, with negligible detrimental impacts on any individual actor (Thouvenin and Tamò-Larrieux 2021).

However, to establish data as a public good, it is key to implement a balanced approach to data access that promotes trust in the digital economy. To enhance this trust, boundaries to the free flow of data must be defined, at least balancing access rights with privacy concerns. In addition to the protection of personal data, certain essential business interests, including trade secrets and other IP rights, should be taken into consideration as well (Thouvenin and Tamò-Larrieux 2021; Noto La Diega and Derclaye 2023). To be effective, this balancing of rights should re-consider traditional conceptualisations of IP, particularly re-evaluating the extent to which IP is actually conducive to innovation and identifying where the over protection of private interests starts to hamper technological progress for the public benefit. Ultimately, facilitating access to data alone will not suffice in fostering innovation if this data cannot legally be utilised (Noto La Diega and Derclaye 2023).

In addition to a general accessibility, unlocking the full potential of big data further requires the free flow of data across borders (Ferracane 2021). This recognition, as well as concomitant obstacles, were emphasized by a Japanese government initiative on 'Data Free Flow with Trust' at the 2019 G20 summit. In this respect, the G20 Osaka Leaders' Declaration summarises: 'Innovation is an important driver for economic growth, which can also contribute to advancing towards the SDGs and enhancing inclusiveness. [...] Cross-border flow of data, information, ideas and knowledge generates higher productivity, greater innovation, and improved sustainable development, while raising challenges related to privacy, data protection, intellectual property rights, and security' (G20 2019). Similar to data lockups at private corporations, the problem in a global context is that governments tend to aim for restrictions of data flows to other countries, as data is regarded as a valuable asset for their domestic industries. Such restrictions of data flows then are liable to hamper innovativeness on a global scale and thus impede the development of products for the public benefit (Burri 2021, Ferracane 2021). On the other hand, particularly when personal data is at stake, the mitigation of legitimate privacy concerns may in fact require certain limitations on permissible data transfers and processing activity in other countries to protect the fundamental rights of domestic data subjects (Burri 2021).

Nonetheless, the UN High-Level Panel on Digital Cooperation emphasized in 2019 that in a global economy that is increasingly reliant on digital interdependence, 'new forms of digital cooperation' are required 'to ensure that digital technologies are built on a foundation of respect for human rights and provide meaningful opportunity for all people and nations' (United Nations 2019 at 6). In a similar vein, the OECD recognises the responsibility of both governments and other stakeholders to facilitate a common digital economy that 'improves peoples' live[s] and boost[s] economic growth for countries at all levels of development, while ensuring that nobody is left behind' (OECD 2018). The free-flow of data across borders is consequently regarded as a highly relevant factor for a fair distribution of value and for facilitating location-independent innovation that serves the public interest globally, potentially contributing to the effective realisation of human rights. In this respect, open data strategies are increasingly implemented and demanded at an international stage by countries of the Global South, which seek to protect their legitimate interests in the technology driven world (Noto La Diega and Derclaye 2023).

Lastly, for the unlocking of big data to be effective, and to enhance its accessibility, it is key to tackle the technical factual power of data holders. In this respect, questions arise as to the quality of data as well as to the portability and interoperability of data sets. Interoperability issues for example arise when technology producers adopt proprietary systems for their data collection and processing that effectively prevent others from utilising the data (Jülicher and Delisle 2018). Facilitating adequate access to data thus requires both the introduction of legal measures that define and regulate questions concerning the ownership of and access rights to data as well as the implementation of means that challenge protectionist technical measures that are liable to thwart the free flow of data.

3 The EU Data Strategy and the Data Act

3.1 The European Data Strategy

Recognising the high value of big data, and the challenges surrounding its utilisation, the EU adopted the Digital Single Market (DSM) Strategy, intending to unlock the economic and social potential of the digital economy. One of the DSM's key aims lies in facilitating the free flow of data to improve its accessibility and utilisation, and to facilitate innovation in the EU (Thouvenin and Tamò-Larrieux 2021; Hennemann and Steinrötter 2022). According to the German Ethics Council it is crucial to recognise the value of data as a social resource (Hornung und Schomberg 2022). One of the key challenges of the digital transformation is to facilitate adequate data access for both individuals and businesses in accordance with fair competition standards, while simultaneously safeguarding the protection of privacy and consumer rights as well as of IP rights. To round-up the potential for value generation from big data, the EU aims to likewise facilitate the transfer of knowledge and data between public and private data holders. Free flow of data is further regarded as a key component of European competitiveness in the global digital economy (Thouvenin and Tamò-Larrieux 2021).

In February 2020, the EU supplemented the DSM by adopting the European Data Strategy which aims at creating the necessary preconditions for a genuine European data economy to establish Europe as a global leader in the digital economy. The Data Act is one of the key pillars of this strategy (COM(2022) 68 final; Specht-Riemenschneider 2022a; Podszun and Pfeifer 2022). As a result of the Covid-19 pandemic, the recovery plan of the EU further recognises that its data strategy needs to establish a data economy that, inter alia, facilitates innovation (SWD(2022) 34 final). In addition to the Data Act, the DSM Strategy and the European Data Strategy rely on a number of legal policies and regulations, including the General Data Protection Regulation (GDPR), the Data Governance Act, the Digital Markets Act, the Digital Services Act, the Artificial Intelligence Act as well as sector specific regulations such as the proposed European Health Data Space (EHDS).

The GDPR provides regulations for the protection of personal data and the fundamental right to privacy of European Citizens, by establishing limitations to the permissible processing of personal data (Regulation (EU) 2016/679). At the core of the Data Governance Act, on the other hand, lie regulations for facilitating the further utilisation and re-use of data held by public sector bodies, for facilitating the mutual utilisation of data between private and public actors, and for furthering data altruism (Hornung and Schomberg 2022). The Data Governance Act further strives to create the necessary preconditions for individuals and corporations to voluntarily share their data without jeopardising their existing rights over this data (COM(2022) 68 final). In particular, the Data Governance Act permits the reuse of certain types of public sector data, even where such data may be commercially confidential or protected by IP rights. This permission, however, is balanced through mechanisms safeguarding the protection of IP, as protected data is strictly shared on the basis of confidentiality (Noto la Diega 2023).

The Digital Markets Act regulates the behaviour of the biggest digital enterprises, i.e. those corporations that provide core platform services while enjoying a “durable and entrenched position”, significantly impacting the European internal market, aiming to prevent them from being gatekeepers of the internet. In comparison to the other regulations of the European digital economy, it is notable that the Digital Markets Act has a strong focus on accessibility while not making any commitments towards the protection of IP (Noto la Diega 2023). The Digital Services Act, on the other hand, promotes responsibilities of private actors towards preventing the abuse of digital services for conducting illegal activities online (Noto la Diega 2023).

While not generally prohibiting high-risk AI systems, the European Artificial Intelligence Act, provides mandatory regulations for their utilisation, requiring transparency to facilitate the appropriate interpretation and use of their output. The main aim of this regulation is to protect the fundamental rights of European citizens in a world where the economy increasingly relies on AI systems that impact technology users, with potentially detrimental consequences (Noto la Diega, 2023).

Lastly, the proposed European Health Data Space provides sector specific regulations for the adequate utilisation of health data. The EDHS is the first proposed sector specific regulation to supplement the Data Act, subject to the Data Acts horizontal regulations (COM(2022) 197 final).

As can be conferred from the amount of different legal policies for the regulation of the European digital economy, one of the core problems of the European Data Strategy is that these different legislative measures regulate different, but also almost all aspects of the data economy. Potentially conflicting targets of these legislative measures, however, are not sufficiently taken into consideration (Veil 2022). The Data Act for example supplements both the Data Governance Act and the GDPR without sufficiently balancing their interrelation with each other (Specht-Riemenschneider 2022a).

3.2 The Data Act

In recognition of the importance of data for the digital economy and for achieving the green and digital transition as well as the fact that data remains under-utilised where its value is held locked-up by a small number of large corporations which hampers the realisation of the full potential of the digital age, on 23 February 2022, the EU introduced a Proposal for a Regulation on harmonised and fair access to and use of data (Data Act, or DA) which aims to establish fairer access to and a fairer value allocation from non-personal data. The proposed Regulation was adopted by the Council on 15 November 2023. Unlocking enclosed data provides immense potential for strengthening a sustainable data economy in

Europe that can reduce the "digital divide" and shall create beneficial opportunities that are available to everyone. To achieve this, data access and its use need to be regulated accordingly. Notably, the European Council explicitly concluded in October 2021 that the regulatory framework for facilitating this accessibility of data shall be conducive to innovation (COM(2022) 68 final at 1). As will be elaborated below, however, the Data Act is unlikely to achieve its goal of creating an environment that enables the full potential of innovativeness as exclusive rights and quasi-exclusive rights that protect data holders remain in place and continue to restrict the accessibility of data for research purposes. The problem of insufficient data access and use for societal purposes is thus not sufficiently mitigated by this regulation.

In March 2021, the European parliament further recognised and highlighted the need for the creation of European data spaces that should enable the free flow of data between different sectors and between public and private stakeholders, including academia (COM(2022) 68 final at 2). While this statement found its way into the Explanatory Memorandum of the Data Act, the Act itself provides no direct data access rights for academia, limiting any public sector access to situations of exceptional need, such as public emergencies (Arts. 14 and 21 DA) or to situations where data access is granted to academia as a third party by request of the user of a device (Art. 5 DA). The European Parliament further highlighted the importance of tackling restrictions of competition, barriers to market entry and broader issues concerning the access and use of data that arise from data enclosures. In this regard, the Data Act aims at facilitating that EU businesses of all sectors receive opportunities through which they can be innovative and competitive (COM(2022) 68 final at 2).

Importantly, the Explanatory Memorandum clarifies that the provisions on data access do not change the scope of previous regulation and protection of data through IP rights, which remain unaltered with the notable exception of the *sui generis* right established by the Database Directive. Similarly, the Data Act will not amend previous European data legislation on sectoral level, but any (future) sectoral legislation should "be aligned with the horizontal principles of the Data Act" (COM(2022) 68 final at 5). In this regard, the Data Act was proposed as a horizontal full-harmonisation regulation that shall provide basic rules applicable to all sectors, so that future sectoral regulation is subject to the general requirements of the Data Act (SWD(2022) 34 final at 7). Therefore, it is to be expected that the Data Act will set the standard for data access rights for the foreseeable future (Specht-Riemenschneider 2022c).

In general, the Data Act pursues the achievement of five targets: (1) facilitating access to and the use of data by consumers and businesses without impeding on incentives for the generation of new data, (2) facilitating the utilisation of data by public sector bodies in situations of exceptional need, (3) facilitating the switching between cloud and edge service providers, (4) providing safeguards against unlawful data transfers by cloud service providers, and (5) providing for the adoption of interoperability standards for data to enhance accessibility (COM(2022) 68 final at 3; From Noto La Diega and Derclaye 2023). The overall objective of the Data Act then lies in maximising the value generation from data for both the economy and society by granting data access to a wider range of stakeholders, facilitating its further use, while balancing these access rights with incentives for the continued collection of new data. Among the specific objectives, the EU further holds that incentives for the sharing of data should facilitate that other businesses can proactively engage in the data economy, which is regarded as a precondition for fostering innovation (SWD(2022) 34 final at 26 and 27).

The now 50 Articles of the Data Act are divided into 11 chapters. Chapter I lays down general provisions, including the scope and subject matter of the data act as well as relevant definitions. Chapters II, III and IV regulate the accessibility and utilisation of data for private actors, including the data holder, users of connected devices and third parties. Chapter V then specifically regulates the access to privately held data by public sector bodies. The regulations provided by Chaps. VI, VII and VIII address specific issues concerning the portability and interoperability of data as well as safeguards for when non-personal data is shared in an international context. While Chaps. IX and XI concern the implementation and enforcement of the Data Act, Chap. X clarifies the relation between the Data Act and the Database Directive by providing limitations to the applicability of the *sui generis* right to database protection. The Data Act shall establish preconditions for facilitating access to data which is generated through the use of connected devices and services. Central to the regulations of the Data Act is thus the creation of mandatory data access rights for both private and business users of connected devices (Specht-Riemenschneider, 2022a). Importantly, the Data Act shall facilitate innovation by opening data enclosures, while maintaining sufficient incentives for the generation of new data (Hennemann and Steinrötter 2022; Podszun and Pfeifer 2022). To achieve the aim of opening data enclosures, the Data Act regulates data accessibility by addressing three main socio-economic dimensions: business to consumer (B2C) relationships, business to business (B2B) relationships, and Business to Government (B2G) relationships (Podszun and Pfeifer 2022).

According to Article 1, the Data Act applies to:

(a) manufacturers of connected products placed on the market in the Union and providers of related services, irrespective of the place of establishment of those manufacturers and providers;
(b) users in the Union of connected products or related services;
(c) data holders, irrespective of their place of establishment, that make data available to data recipients in the Union;
(d) data recipients in the Union to whom data are made available;
(e) public sector bodies, the Commission, the European Central Bank and Union bodies that request data holders to make data available where there is an exceptional need for those data for the performance of a specific task carried out in the public interest and to the data holders that provide those data in response to such request; (f) providers of data processing services, irrespective of their place of establishment, providing such services to customers in the Union; (g) participants in data spaces and vendors of applications using smart contracts and persons whose trade, business or profession involves the deployment of smart contracts for others in the context of executing an agreement (Art. 1(3) DA).

Notably, similar to the applicability of the GDPR, the Data Act follows the *lex loci solutionis* principle, meaning that its applicability is subject to the relevant marketplace. In other words, the regulations of the Data Act apply to all data holders when data is generated within the European market (Hennemann and Steinrötter 2022). Additionally,

Article 1(5) DA provides that the Data Act is without prejudice to the applicability of EU data privacy and data protection laws, and that the access rights of Chap. II of the Data Act shall supplement the access and portability rights of the GDPR. Considering, however, that user generated data in many instances is likely to be of personal nature, the Data Act leaves various tensions between data access and data protection largely unresolved (Kerber 2022).

Article 2 DA provides definitions that apply for the purposes of the regulation. Here, data is defined as "any digital representation of acts, facts or information and any compilation of such acts, facts or information, including in the form of sound, visual or audio-visual recording" (Art. 2(1) DA). The term data is thus not simply regarded as synonymous to the term information but is rather regarded as a means for transporting information (Hennemann and Steinrötter 2022). Notably, storage devices and mere online services are *a priori* excluded from the scope of the Data Act (Specht-Riemenschneider 2022b). Furthermore, recital 15 specifically excludes derivative data – i.e. data that results from the processing or analysis of raw data – from the regulations of the Data Act (Recital 15 DA). This exclusion is particularly regrettable as raw data can often be too limited to be re-usable, while the re-use of derivative data could provide valuable insights, benefitting research for societal purposes (Podszun and Pfeifer 2022). In contrast to raw data, however, the creation of derivative data requires an effort by the data holder and may thus be protected by IP rights. Where such data is not protected by IP rights, the Data Act may then strengthen the exclusive position of data holders in the future. For achieving the aim of promoting innovation towards sustainability and the common good, however, it is key that adequate data accessibility is designed in a way that facilitates the unlocking of the full value of big data (Noto La Diega and Derclaye 2023).

3.2.1 B2B and B2C Data Access

According to Article 3 DA, products are to be designed in a way that facilitates easy direct product data and related service data accessibility for their users (accessibility by design), provided that such direct access is secure and appropriate (Art. 3 DA). However, a mere direct accessibility of data may not be sufficient in that the regulation leaves unclear whether providing *in-situ* access can suffice to fulfil this accessibility requirement (Podszun and Pfeifer 2022). When read in conjunction with Article 4 DA and recitals 8 and 22, it seems data holders can fulfil their obligations by simply providing online data access without being required to share a copy of the relevant data (Kerber 2022). While *in-situ* access may seem like an adequate safeguard to mitigate the risks of unnecessary data transfers, this limitation can also provide an easy pretext for data holders to circumvent the actual sharing of their data (Kerber 2022; Podszun and Pfeifer 2022). In addition to the accessibility by design requirement, Article 3(2) and (3) DA introduce a transparency requirement that shall protect the interests of users by enabling them to make informed decisions on the processing of their generated data before they enter into a contract with the data holder (Hennemann and Steinrötter 2022).

Articles 4 and 5 DA provide users of connected devices with non-waivable rights that facilitate the accessibility and sharing of their generated data for all legal purposes, subject to certain limitations (Kerber 2022). While Article 3 DA establishes the accessibility by design requirement, Article 4 provides both private and business users of connected devices with a direct right against the producer to access and use their generated data, if the producer is also the data holder (Art. 4(1) DA). The aim of this right is to make data accessible to the users whose usage of a device is a key component for the production of this data. In relation to the GDPR, it is important to note that according to recital 7, the data access right of Article 4 DA does not create a new legal basis permitting the processing of personal data (Hennemann and Steinrötter 2022). The control of users is further strengthened by Article 4(13) DA, providing that the data holder may only process user generated data on a contractual agreement with the user (Art. 4(13) DA). At a first glance, this may be regarded as an attribution of the data ownership to the user, as the data holder can only realise the data's economic value with the user's consent (Hennemann and Steinrötter 2022). In reality, however, this hurdle is easy to overcome for data holders as distinct guidelines for consumer protection applicable to relevant contractual terms are missing. This problem can already be observed with respect to informed consent under the regulation of the GDPR, where, due to information asymmetries, data subjects often struggle to understand what they are consenting to exactly. Similarly, the current text of the Data Act does not prevent the data holder from implementing buy-out contracts by which the user consent becomes an integral part of the purchase or leasing contract of a device (Specht- Riemenschneider 2022a, b; Podszun and Pfeifer 2022).

Taking account of potential conflicts between data access rights and IP rights, Article 4(6) DA clarifies that data access cannot be denied for reasons of trade secrecy, but that instead measures need to put in place that sufficiently protect trade secrets, for example through the conclusion of an NDA (Art. 4(6) DA; Hennemann and Steinrötter 2022). However, Article 4(8) DA provides that in exceptional circumstances where the trade secret holder can "demonstrate the high probability of suffering serious economic damage from the disclosure of trade secrets, despite the technical and organisational measures taken by the user", data access by the user can be refused on a case-by-case basis (Art. 4(8) DA). To protect the legitimate interests of data holders, Article 4(10) DA prevents users from utilising the accessed data for the development of competing products (Art. 4(10) DA). While this prohibition may restrict activities that could lead to the development of improved products and enhance competition, it also provides a reasonable limitation to access rights so that the initial developers of innovative products are not disincentivised from being innovative (Podszun and Pfeifer 2022).

In accordance with recital 5, Article 5 DA facilitates that users cannot only access and use their data themselves, but further share this data with third parties or request that a third party receives direct access to the user data from the data holder (Art. 5 DA, Recital 5 DA). However, the Data Act does not establish a general direct access right for third parties (Specht-Riemenschneider 2022a). Data access by third parties is thus dependent on the willingness of the user to grant such access (Hennemann and Steinrötter 2022). While this restriction of third-party access is adequate from a consumer protection perspective, it also severely limits the facilitation of the re-use of data for research purposes (Specht-Riemenschneider 2022b). Similar to Article 4(6), Article 5(9) DA provides safeguards for trade secrets of the data holder. In general, it can be observed that the Data Act prioritises access rights over trade secret protection, as long as sufficient measures are taken to preserve their confidentiality (Specht-Riemenschneider 2022c). With respect to third-party data transfers, however, the data holder is only required to disclose trade secrets "to the extent that such disclosure is strictly necessary to fulfil the purpose agreed between the user and the third party" (Art. 5(9) DA).

This prioritisation of data access over trade secrets is later somewhat mitigated by Art 8(6) DA which provides that "an obligation to make data available to a data recipient shall not oblige the disclosure of trade secrets" unless specifically provided for by Union law or the national implementation of Union law (Art. 8(6) DA). Article 11 DA then provides safeguards for data holders, enabling them to implement technical measures such as smart contracts and encryption to ensure that the shared data is not accessed or used in an unlawful manner by third parties (Art. 11(1) DA).

Such protection is particularly important for safeguarding the confidentiality of trade secrets, as even where conventional protection for trade secrets is in place, its enforceability can be jeopardised once a secret has been made public. Smart contracts mitigate this risk by enabling the data holder to gain insights into if and how the shared data was used by third parties (Bartke et al. 2022). Article 11(2) and (3) DA provide further defensive rights for data holders against the illegitimate utilisation of their data which strengthens their de-facto exclusive position. This may potentially lead to an over protection of the data (Specht-Riemenschneider 2022b). While implementing technical safeguards is generally a reasonable measure for protecting the legitimate interests of data holders, a potential abuse of smart contracts, however, may be liable to hamper the utilisation of shared data for innovation purposes.

Strengthening the position of the user toward third parties, Article 6 DA provides that third parties shall only process the data they receive under Article 5 subject to purposes and conditions agreed upon with the user (Art. 6(1) DA). The user decides thus not only *if* and *with whom* they want to share their generated data, but also *what* the data can be used for by third parties. While this is again a welcome inclusion of consumer protection measures, a purpose limitation for the use of non-personal data can adversely impact innovativeness, as research may discover new, previously unknown purposes for utilising such data to achieve societal objectives. Similar to the limitation of the usage rights of users, Art 6(2)(e) further restricts innovative activity by preventing third parties from using data received via the user for developing products that are in competition with the products and services of the data holder from which the data originates (Art. 6(2)(e) DA). Additionally, the purpose limitation is supplemented with further safeguards, including a prohibition for the third party to share the user data with another third party, or better a fourth party, unless this is necessary for the delivery of services commissioned by the user (Art. 6(2)(c) DA). To protect free competition on the European Single Market, Article 6(2)(d) DA specifically prevents users from sharing data they receive from the data holder with third parties who, according to the Digital Markets Act, are designated as gatekeepers to prevent those gatekeepers from further strengthening their market positions by gaining data from competitors via their users (Art. 6(2)(d) DA).

Even when a user decides to share their generated data with a third party, to utilise this data the third party is required to enter into two contractual relationships both with the user and with the data holder. In other words, a user cannot directly share their data with the third party without a licensing agreement between the third party and the data holder. A third party who intends to use data for research and innovation may also require access to aggregated datasets. The requirement to have contractual relations with the data holder and each individual user, however, makes acquiring aggregated datasets not just difficult, but potentially impossible. Therefore, the regulations for third party access in the Data Act fail in establishing necessary preconditions for facilitating meaningful innovation (Kerber 2022).

To prevent data holders from abusing their factual control over the data and to mitigate power imbalances in contract negotiations, Article 8(1) DA provides that data shall be made accessible to users and third parties on fair, reasonable and non-discriminatory (FRAND) terms (Art. 8(1) DA; Hennemann and Steinrötter 2022). While according to Article 9, the data holder can require a reasonable payment for data transfers, the data holder cannot freely determine the fees and conditions for data access by third parties (Kerber 2022). For small and medium-sized enterprises (SMEs) and non-profit organisations fees are even limited to the actual costs incurred by making the data available (Art. 9(4) DA). In general, the Data Act seems to emphasize the specific needs of small enterprises, as Article 7 DA completely exempts data holders who qualify as small and micro enterprises according to Union law from the B2C and B2B data sharing requirements, provided that they are not linked to other enterprises or partner organisations (Art. 7 DA).

3.2.2 B2G Data Access

In addition to the B2C and B2B data access rights, chapter V of the Data Act provides a direct data access entitlement for the public sector, i.e. public sector bodies or Union Institutions, agencies and bodies. The main regulation facilitating public sector access, Article 14 DA, however, strictly limits the access right to situations of exceptional need (Art. 14 DA). Article 15 DA then defines that an exceptional need to use data shall be limited in time and scope, and only exists in circumstances:

(a) where the data requested is necessary to respond to a public emergency and the public sector body, the Commission, the European Central Bank or the Union body is unable to obtain such data by alternative means in a timely and effective manner under equivalent conditions;
(b) in circumstances not covered by point (a) and only insofar as non-personal data is concerned, where:

  (i) a public sector body, the Commission, the European Central Bank or a Union body is acting on the basis of Union or national law and has identified specific data, the lack of which prevents it from fulfilling a specific task carried out in the public interest, that has been explicitly provided for by law, such as the production of official statistics or the mitigation of or recovery from a public emergency; and
  (ii) the public sector body, the Commission, the European Central Bank or the Union body has exhausted all other means at its disposal to obtain such data, including purchase of non-personal data on the market by offering market rates, or by relying

on existing obligations to make data available or the adoption of new legislative measures which could guarantee the timely availability of the data (Art. 15 DA).

Article 17 DA provides further administrative requirements for data requests by public bodies. The restrictive requirements of Articles 15 and 17 seem to be designed to make data access by governments a rare exception (Specht-Riemenschneider, 2022c). And even where governments gain access to user generated data, the utilisation of such data is subject to further strict limitations under Article 19 DA, including a purpose limitation, so that shared data can only be used to respond to the situation of exceptional need and must be destroyed once it is no longer required for achieving that purpose (Art. 19(1) DA).

While Article 21 DA facilitates that data accessed by public sector bodies can be further shared with non-profit organisations that conduct scientific research with a public interest mission, this right is similarly limited to the purposes for which the data was initially requested, meaning the research can only be conducted to respond to the specific exceptional circumstances (Art. 21 DA). One of the aims of granting public sector access is to make it easier for public sector bodies to obtain and re-use privately held data for public interest purposes (SWD(2022) 34 final Annex 3). A limitation to situations of exceptional need is thus too narrow. In this regard, it is particularly regrettable that there is no direct access right for public research institutions outside of situations of exceptional need. To adequately unlock data enclosures, thereby facilitating meaningful and swift innovation, access to data is required on situation-independent basis. On the other hand, limitations for government access to data may nonetheless be important to mitigate the risk that governments obtain a general opportunity to evaluate and analyse product data in an abusive manner to the detriment of their citizens (Podszun and Pfeifer, 2022).

3.2.3 International Data Transfers, Interoperability Standards, and the Sui Generis Right

Article 32 DA provides regulations and safeguards concerning international access to and transfer of data. In particular, these regulations aim to protect data held within the EU from unlawful access by international actors and governments if such access would be in conflict with Union law or the law of EU Member States (Art. 32(1) DA). The regulations provide an additional layer of protection for non-personal data, as international transfers of personal data are already regulated by the GDPR. While, if adequately applied, the regulations of Article 32 protect the rights and interests of European data holders and users of connected devices, international data flows are also an important driver for innovation and a requirement for a fair value allocation in the global digital economy. It is therefore crucial that any restrictions to the free flow of data are sufficiently balanced.

To unlock data enclosures and to facilitate the adequate accessibility of data, it is important that data can be utilised by the recipients of shared data without the requirement of substantial additional investments. In this respect, Article 33 DA introduces essential requirements that operators of data spaces need to fulfil to facilitate the interoperability of their data (Art. 33 DA). These requirements should make it easier for actors other than the data holder to find relevant data and reduce transaction costs for when the data is shared and re-used (SWD(2022) 34 final at 27). Thereby, the sharing of different types of data between different providers shall be made possible, which, in turn, shall facilitate the creation of common data spaces in strategic sectors for the public benefit (Podszun and Pfeifer 2022).

Lastly, the Data Act recognises at least some of the potentially detrimental impacts of IP rights on the sharing of data. In this regard, Article 43 DA explicitly excludes the applicability of the *sui generis* right of Article 7 of the Database Directive for data obtained from the use of connected devices to prevent the Database Directive from jeopardising the effectiveness of the Data Act (Art. 43 DA).

3.2.4 Initial Critique of the Data Act

All things considered, there seems to be a consensus among scholars and commentators that the Data Act is unlikely to achieve its goals. In particular, it is suggested that the Data Act, as well as the other EU policies on the digital economy, fail in providing sufficient preconditions for facilitating open access to data (Noto La Diega and Derclaye 2023). The Commission Staff Impact Assessment Report accompanying the Data Act suggests that "the Data Act would enable wider data use across the economy, notably by regulating the fundamental questions of who can use the data generated by connected products and related services, and what are the conditions for such use." (SWD(2022) 34 final) As this is supposed to facilitate consumer choice and promote innovation, it is regrettable that considerations of public research are not sufficiently included in the legislation. A limitation, or better exception, allowing business-to-government data access, including for public research purposes, only in exceptional situations is simply too narrow to foster any meaningful innovation for the public benefit. Recognising that in accordance with the Data Governance Act, public data is made available for re-use by private corporations, it seems reasonable to suggest that a similar general access right for the public to utilise data held by enterprises for societal objectives should be considered (Thouvenin and Tamò-Larrieux 2021; Noto La Diega and Derclaye 2023).

Furthermore, the Data Act, and the European Data Strategy more generally, do not conclusively resolve conflicts between openness requirements and property rights. While in essence, through the Data Act, the EU rejects the idea of a *de jure* property right to data, new safeguards are implemented that consolidate property-like positions of data holders (Hennemann and Steinrötter 2022; Kerber 2022; Noto la Diega 2023; Podszun and Pfeifer 2022). Thereby, the Data Act effectively strengthens the technical-factual control of the data holder. Open data access thus only exists on paper but is negated by the various limitations of the Data Act (Veil 2022; Specht-Riemenschneider 2022a, b). The technical-factual control of the data holder is thus the general rule supported by the Data Act, which is only restricted in the exceptional circumstances that a user utilises their data access rights (Specht-Riemenschneider, 2022c). As the data holder remains in control over the data, it seems that any access is an exception which requires a justification. Conversely, it should be questioned whether it is not the quasi-exclusive control of the data holder that requires a justification in the first place (Specht-Riemenschneider 2022a, b). As long as the law accepts the technical-factual control of the data holder as the default position, the Data Act cannot achieve its aim of unlocking large amounts of data for innovation purposes. The access and sharing rights are too limited and thus too weak while the effective control of the data holder is strengthened (Kerber 2022). In particular, data holders gain the potential to delay or even prevent data access by third parties, with long negotiations and potential disputes hampering swift access for innovation purposes (Podszun and Pfeifer 2022).

All things considered, the Data Act's acceptance of the de facto control of data holders strengthens their position with legal entitlements which are similar to the exclusive rights provided by IP protection, making access an exception to the norm. The Data Act thus urgently requires rebalancing as a legally accepted de-facto control provides data holders with a quasi-exclusive right to data, which in turn may consolidate potential monopolistic market positions (Kerber 2022).

4 A de-Facto Exclusive Right to Data

By enabling the creation of monopolies or monopolistic market positions for rights holders, the granting of exclusive rights constitutes a restriction of the free competition principle. In the intellectual property debate, and in consideration of the social contract theory, the restriction of competition through exclusive rights is arguably justified by the incentives they provide for innovativeness with potential public benefits. Investors are incentivised by receiving an opportunity to profit from risky investments, or at least a chance to recover their R&D investments (Bartke et al. 2022). The granting of exclusive rights under IP laws is not uncontroversial and was heavily criticised over the past decades. In particular, it can be suggested that in vital sectors, such as health, the public benefits of innovation are negated by exclusive rights that facilitate monopolistic market positions and lead to higher prices. To be justified, it is thus crucial to ensure that exclusive rights are adequately balanced as any overprotection would negatively tip the balance between the legitimate interests of inventors or investors and the interests of society at large in favour of the former.

Additionally, balanced IP regulations, or the regulation of non-scarce resources more generally, need to be adapted to current economic and scientific conditions. Historically, when IP laws were first introduced, innovation was considered a closed process, meaning that the innovative process was entirely conducted by a single inventor or at least within the confinements of a single enterprise. However, the approach to innovation has changed over the past decades and an opening of the innovative process, by which corporations increasingly rely on external knowledge, can be observed. This trend, suitably termed open innovation, reflects the increasing reliance of innovators on cooperation rather than competition, which enhances and accelerates innovation processes for the benefit of all stakeholders (Bartke et al. 2022). The transition towards open innovation calls into question whether traditional IP systems and their reliance on the provision of exclusive rights remain fit for their purpose in an open innovation environment. The experience with Covid-19 and the accelerated development of vaccines highlights the crucial importance of open innovation, as access to health and research data was key for responding to the pandemic in a timely manner, particularly when compared to the regular duration required for the development of new medicines. On the other hand, industry may claim that in an open innovation context, there is actually a growing need for protection of the interests of those who invest in data generation, to incentives the sharing of such data by mitigating detrimental impacts on investors and by clarifying current legal uncertainties (Bartke et al. 2022).

Similar to the experience with IP rights, the de-facto control over data can impede on free market dynamics. When a data holder has the control over an extensive data set generated by their products and can exponentially increase this "data treasure" by exclusively utilising the data to develop improved products and thereby surpass all competition, the data holder may end up in a monopolistic position on the market. This is detrimental to the market entry and innovativeness of competitors. An adequate stimulation of innovativeness would thus require adequate access to this data by third parties (Bartke et al. 2022). Broad access rights to such data would be comparable to regulations for standard essential patents (SEPs), access to which is required even where the patent holder is unwilling to voluntarily grant a license. To tackle this problem, SEP holders are now required to grand licenses to everyone on FRAND terms (Bartke et al. 2022). While the Data Act specifically includes a reference to FRAND terms in Article 8, in contrast to SEPs, there still exists no general data access right for third parties. The limitations provided by the Data Act rather strengthen the position of data holders vis-à-vis competitors who require data access, consolidating their exclusive position.

4.1 The Problem with Exclusivity: Lessons from the Global Harmonisation of Intellectual Property Rights

As the arguments for a de facto control of data holders are quite similar to the debates concerning patent rights, the following analysis shall exemplify the conflict between exclusive rights and innovation by reference to a notable experience that emerged from the international harmonisation of minimum patent protection standards through the WTO TRIPS Agreement. One of the main arguments for introducing patent rights for all fields of technology, including the pharmaceutical sector, in countries, and particularly developing countries that formerly did not provide for the patentability of pharmaceuticals was that patents provide inventors with an incentive for being innovative. The premise of stronger global patent protection was then to increase encouragement for the development of new medicines, including products that serve the interests of the developing world. Particularly in the field of pharmaceuticals, the development of new products involves substantially high costs and are regarded as a high-risk investment (Abbott 2015; ECOSOC 2001; Hestermeyer 2007; Reichman 2009). Granting exclusive rights via the provision of patents should then incentivise high risk investments by facilitating the successful commercialisation of new medicines through the provision of time-limited monopoly positions on the markets (Abbott 2011; Flynn et al. 2009). As tackling global disease burdens not only requires the affordability of existing medications, but also the future availability of new medicines, it can be argued that limited exclusive rights provide a balance between the interests of industry and the wider societal interests (Abbott 2015; Henry and Searles 2012; Phillips 2006).

While it may be true that an adequate level of patent protection can be beneficial for stimulating innovation, overly strong or excessive protection may in fact have detrimental impacts on innovation by creating new obstacles for future research activity. As innovation is frequently the result of research activity that builds upon prior discoveries, a stringent patent protection of older inventions is liable to prevent researchers from utilising existing knowledge, thereby delaying future innovation (Abbott 2015; Richards 2008; Smith et al. 2009). A continuous proliferation of patent protection therefore directly contradicts its very purpose of stimulating innovation by restricting the innovative activity of competitors. The exclusive rights granted under patent protection thus can be used to effectively hinder innovation (Richards 2008; ECOSOC 2001). This concern is particularly prevalent in the pharmaceutical sector, where the development of an administrable medicine is the result of several stages of innovation. As each of these stages can potentially suffice for fulfilling patentability requirements, the granting of patents can create further obstacles for researchers who cannot utilise the results of previous development steps if a competitor receives exclusive protection (ECOSOC 2001). By restricting opportunities for utilising existing knowledge, the exclusive rights granted to patentees are therefore liable to ultimately delay technological progress (Richards 2008). By and large, it can be summarised that the global introduction of pharmaceutical patent rights created new obstacles that hamper appropriate research efforts, thereby defeating the very purposes for which they were introduced. Adding a new layer to this protection by consolidating quasi-exclusive rights for data holders of user generated raw data, particularly from smart health devices, would in all probability create further obstacles, aggravating the already problematic situation.

4.2 An Exclusive Right to Data and the Problem of IP Overlaps

In the modern digital economy, the introduction of a quasi-exclusive right to data would further considerably strengthen the defensive position and strategy of rights holders, who can rely on their data rights in a worrying synergy with other IP rights. This synergy lies in the potential overlapping of exclusive protection. Just as in the traditional regulation of IP rights, the Data Act effectively provides for access rights, and particularly public and third-party access, as an exception to the general rule. Notably, each regulation of the different types of IP and data rights has its own permissibility requirements for granting exceptions. This becomes particularly problematic, where different exclusive rights cover the same substance. In today's economy, there exists a "growing fusion between hardware, software, digital content, services, data and biotechnologies." (Noto La Diega and Derclaye 2023). A single product may, for example, enjoy protection of various patents, trademarks, trade secrets and now, potentially include a de facto control of the data. The exceptions to each of these rights are quite specific, and similar exceptions for the same exceptional reasons may not be enshrined in the regulation of another right. An exception for public health reasons under patent laws, for example, may not exist in the same manner under trademark law or trade secret protection. When multi-IP protection exists, the exceptions of each individual set of rights may thus become insufficient when the rights holder can rely on another right to maintain their protection. While a legitimate exception under patent rights would facilitate access, the non-existence of an equivalent exception could render such access nevertheless an infringement of trademark or trade secrecy laws (Noto La Diega and Derclaye 2023; Noto La Diega 2022a). An exclusive rights system that subjects access rights to specific exceptions thus faces the risk that other exclusive rights may remain in place, restricting adequate and legitimate accessibility. Ultimately, the more stringent exclusive protection systems are liable to prevail, thereby diminishing the efficacy of exceptions provided by systems that are more generous towards access (Noto La Diega and Derclaye 2023).

As the Explanatory Memorandum to the Data Act provides that IP rights remain unaltered, the Data Act leaves potential conflicts between IP and data accessibility unresolved, or better excludes it from its focus (COM(2022) 68 final at 5; Noto La Diega and Derclaye 2023). By suggesting that the Data Act is without prejudice to IP rights and trade secret protection the regulation aims to guarantee the continued protection of rights holders (SWD(2022) 34 final Annex 8). While it is sensible to suggest that the legal rights of IP owners generally should be protected, in respect to data access, it is also clear that IP rights impact innovation in different ways, and not just by providing incentives for investments. When aiming to unlock data for innovation purposes, existing problems with IP protection standards should therefore be taken into deeper consideration. Attempting to regulate data access while ignoring the pre-existing issues arising from stringent IP protection is simply insufficient.

Thus, while the general premise of enhancing data access through the Data Act is good, IP needs to be accounted for to enable meaningful innovation. The categorical exclusion of IP considerations from the Data Act does nothing to mitigate current legal uncertainties. Rather, it creates new uncertainties where the laws and their teleological purposes stand in conflict. Accordingly, the consolidation of a quasi-exclusive position of data holders is likely to aggravate the already existing problems of exclusive IP rights, where access is merely side-lined to the exceptions.

5 Conclusion

This chapter has highlighted the importance of big data for the modern digital economy and particularly the crucial importance of facilitating access to data to enhance meaningful innovation toward societal objectives. Section 3 has introduced the European strategy on how data can be used more efficiently, including consideration of how access for the various stakeholders shall be facilitated. In this respect, this contribution took a deeper look at the initial proposal of the Data Act that shall establish fairer access to and a fairer value allocation from non-personal data. The unlocking of data enclosures shall thereby strengthen a sustainable data economy in Europe, creating beneficial opportunities for everyone. Notably, the accessibility and utilisation of data shall be regulated in a manner that is conducive to innovation. As elaborated in this contribution, however, the Data Act is unlikely to achieve its objectives.

It is welcome that the Data Act introduces safeguards that prevent gatekeepers from profiting from data access rights and utilising their power to gain access to further data, while at the same time recognising the specific needs of small and micro enterprises and start-ups (Podszun and Pfeifer 2022). Similarly commendable is that the Data Act introduces interoperability requirements to facilitate the creation of common data spaces to enhance the re-usability of data. To re-use data in the first place, however, stakeholders require adequate access rights. This is where the Data Act is likely to fail. In the outset, this contributions questions whether the Data Act is successful in striking an adequate balance between the rights and obligations of the various stakeholders. Upon close examination, it can be observed that while the Data Act aims at facilitating the access and re-use of data, the specific regulations that grant access rights are limited by a number of conditions. While it may be relatively easy for the user of connected decides to gain access to their created data, it is likely that a mere *in-situ* access suffices to fulfil the requirements of the Data Act. As the user then would not receive a copy of their data, the re-use of such data would be hampered. Data access is further complicated for third parties who have an interest in utilising the data for innovation purposes or for the provision of after market services. Access for third parties is dependent on the willingness of either the data holder or the specific user. A general access right for third parties is non-existent. If access is granted by a user, the third party is further required to enter contractual agreements both with the data holder and with each individual user, which makes the acquisition of aggregated datasets for third parties almost impossible. Such aggregated datasets, however, would be required for fostering meaningful innovation. For the data collector, on the other hand, the limitations to the access rights in the Data Act imply that even though the EU rejects the concept of a legal property right to data, the Data Act strengthens the de facto control of the data holder. Thereby, the Data Act grants the data holder a quasi-exclusive position.

This leads us to the second question raised by this chapter of whether the Data Act provides for sufficient accessibility of data to facilitate its re-use for innovation activity towards societal objectives. The answer to this question likewise is negative. The quasi-exclusive de facto control, and the fact that third parties have no direct access right to data, provides data holders with the opportunity to prevent or delay access to such data for research purposes. This position is particularly strong, where a product resulting from research activity may stand in competition with the product from which the raw data originates. More important from a public interest perspective, however, is that the Data Act does not establish a general access right for academia or other public research institutions. Any access by the public sector is limited to situations of exceptional need. This is regrettable, particularly when considering that the Data Governance Act makes publicly held data available for commercial exploitation by private enterprises. A similar access right for the public to utilise privately held data for societal objectives therefore would be desirable. All in all, it seems that the Data Act trips over the same pitfalls as modern international IP protection standards when it comes to regulating access rights. So, while the Data Act is an urgently required valuable step in the right direction, to be adequate for regulating the modern digital economy, its provisions require further re-balancing. In particular, the limitations to access rights should be re-calibrated to ensure that data accessibility provides a proportionate counterbalance to the de facto control of data holders to prevent the introduction of a legally accepted quasi-exclusive right to data.

References

Aaronson, S. A. (2021). Data is Different, so Policymakers should pay Close Attention to its Governance. In M. Burri (Ed.), *Big Data and Global Trade Law* (pp. 340–359) Cambridge University Press

Abbott, F.M. (2011). Intellectual Property and Public Health: Meeting the Challenge of Sustainability. Global Health Programme Working Paper No7/2011. Retrieved December 12, 2023, from https://papers.ssrn.com/sol3/papers.cfm?abstract_id=1965458

Abbott, F.M. (2015). Trade in Medicines. In R. Smith et al. (eds), *Trade and Health: Towards Building a National Strategy* (pp. 117–136) World Health Organization

Bartke, L. et al. (2022). Der Schutz von Trainingsdaten de lege ferenda: What would Machlup do? *RDi Recht Digital*, 431–439

Burri, M. (2021). Data Flows and Global Trade Law. In M. Burri (Ed.), *Big Data and Global Trade Law* (pp. 11–41) Cambridge University Press

Culik, N. (2018). Brussels Calling: Big Data and Privacy. In T. Hoeren, & B. Kolany-Raiser (Eds.), *Big Data in Context: Legal, Social and Technological Insights* (pp. 29–35) Springer Nature

Drexl, J. et al. (2016). Data Ownership and Access to Data – Position Statement of the Max Planck Institute for Innovation and Competition of 16 August 2016 on the Current European Debate. *Max Planck Institute for Innovation & Competition Research Paper No. 16–10.* Retrieved December 12, 2023, from http://dx.doi.org/10.2139/ssrn.2833165

Ferracane, M. F. (2021). The Cost of Data Protectionism. In M. Burri (Ed.), *Big Data and Global Trade Law* (pp. 63–82) Cambridge University Press

Flynn, S., Hollis A. and Palmedo M. (2009). An Economic Justification for Open Access to Essential Medicine Patents in Developing Countries. *37 Journal of Law, Medicine & Ethics*, 184–208

G20, (2019, June 29). *G20 Osaka Leaders' Declaration*. Retrieved December 12, 2023, from https://www.consilium.europa.eu/media/40124/final_g20_osaka_leaders_declaration.pdf

Gervais, D. J. (2021). TRIPS Meets Big Data. In M. Burri (Ed.), *Big Data and Global Trade Law* (pp. 160–176) Cambridge University Press

Hennemann, M. & Steinrötter, B. (2022). Data Act – Fundament des neuen EU-Datenwirtschaftsrechts? *NJW Neue Jusristische Wochenschrift*, 1481–1486

Henry, D. and Searles, A. (2012). Chapter 9: Pharmaceutical Pricing Policy. In Management Sciences for Health (ed.) *MDS-3: Managing Access to Medicines and Health Technologies* (at 9.2–9.22) 3rd edn, Management Sciences for Health

Hestermeyer, H. (2007) *Human Rights and the WTO: The Case of Patents and Access to Medicines*. Oxford University Press

Hornung, G. and Schomberg, S. (2022). Datensouveränität im Spannungsfeld zwischen Datenschutz und Datenzugang: das Beispiel des Data Governance Acts. *Computer und Recht*, 508–516

Irion, K. (2021). Panta Rhei: A European Perspective on Ensuring a High Level of Protection of Human Rights in a World in Which Everything Flows. In M. Burri (Ed.), *Big Data and Global Trade Law* (pp. 231–242) Cambridge University Press

Jülicher, T. (2018). Education 2.0: Learning Analytics, Educational Data Mining and Co. In T. Hoeren, & B. Kolany-Raiser (Eds.), *Big Data in Context: Legal, Social and Technological Insights* (pp. 47–53) Springer Nature

Jülicher, T. and Delisle M. (2018). Step into „The Circle" – A Close Look at Wearables and Quantified Self. In T. Hoeren, & B. Kolany-Raiser (Eds.), *Big Data in Context: Legal, Social and Technological Insights* (pp. 81–91) Springer Nature

Kerber, W. (2022). Governance of IoT Data: Why the EU Data Act Will not Fulfill Its Objectives. *GRUR International, 72*(2), 120–135

Manyyika, J. et al. (2016). *Digital Globalisation: The New Era of Global Flows*. McKinsey Global Institute

Noto La Diega, G. (2022a). *Internet of Things and the Law: Legal Strategies for Consumer-Centric Smart Technologies*. Routledge

Noto La Diega, G. (2022b, November 04). *New chapter! "Ending Smart Data Enclosures: The European Approach to the Regulation of the Internet of Things between Access and Intellectual Property*. Blog post retrieved December 12, 2023, from https://guidonotoladiega.wordpress.com/2022/11/04/new-chapter-ending-smart-data-enclosures-the-european-approach-to-the-regulation-of-the-internet-of-things-between-access-and-intellectual-property/

Noto La Diega, G. (2023). Ending Smart Data Enclosures: The European Approach to the Regulation of the Internet of Things between Access and Intellectual Property. In S.-A. Elvy and N. Kim (Eds.), *The Cambridge Handbook on Emerging Issues at the Intersection of Commercial Law and Technology* (Forthcoming) Cambridge University Press

Noto La Diega, G. and Derclaye, E. (2023). Opening Up Big Data for Sustainability: What Role for Database Rights in the Fourth Industrial Revolution? In O.-A. Rognstad et al. (Eds.), *Promoting Sustainable Innovation and the Circular Economy: Legal and Economic Aspects* (Forthcoming) Routledge

OECD. (2018). *Going Digital in a Multilateral World: An Interim Report to Ministers, Executive Summary Meeting of the Council at Ministerial Level, 30–31 May 2018*. Retrieved December 12, 2023, from http://www.oecd.org/mcm/documents/C-MIN-2018-6-EN.pdf?utm_source=Adestra&utm_medium=email&utm_content=Read%20the%20report%20here...&utm_campaign=OECD%20Going%20Digital%20News%20-June%202018&utm_term=demo

Phillips A.A. (2006). Strengthen Pharmaceutical Patent Rights: Lowering the Cost of Prescription Drugs by Stopping the Reckless Patent Litigation Abuse of Generic Companies. *13 Connecticut Insurance Law Journal*, 397–426

Podszun, R. and Pfeifer, C. (2022). Datenzugang nach dem EU Data Act: Der Entwurf der Europäischen Kommission. *Gewerblicher Rechtsschutz und Urheberrecht*, 953–961

Regulation (EU) 2016/679 of the European Parliament and of the Council of 27 April 2016 on the protection of natural persons with regard to the processing of personal data and on the free movement of such data, and repealing Directive 95/46/EC (General Data Protection Regulation). Retrieved December 12, 2023, from https://eur-lex.europa.eu/legal-content/EN/TXT/PDF/?uri=CELEX:32016R0679

Reichman, J.H. (2009). Comment: Compulsory Licensing of Patented Pharmaceutical Inventions: Evaluating the Options. *37 Journal of Law, Medicine & Ethics*, 247–263

Richards, D.G. (2008). A Skeptik's View of Intellectual Property Rights. In R.C. Bird & S.C. Jain (eds), *The Global Challenge of Intellectual Property Rights* (pp. 267–282) Edward Elgar Publishing

Röttgen, C. (2018). Like or Dislike – Web Tracking. In T. Hoeren, & B. Kolany-Raiser (Eds.), *Big Data in Context: Legal, Social and Technological Insights* (pp. 73–79) Springer Nature

Seuba, X. (2021). Big Data, AI and Border Enforcement of Intellectual Property Rights. In M. Burri (Ed.), *Big Data and Global Trade Law* (pp. 177–192) Cambridge University Press.

Smith, R.D., Correa, C. and Oh, C. (2009). Trade, TRIPS, and Pharmaceuticals. *373 The Lancet*, 684-691

Specht-Riemenschneider, L. (2022a). Der Entwurf des Data Act: Ein großer Wurf in die falsche Richtung? *GRUR Gewerblicher Rechtsschutz und Urheberrecht*, 937–938

Specht-Riemenschneider, L. (2022b). Data Act – Auf dem (Holz-)Weg zu mehr Dateninnovation? *Zeitschrift für Rechtspolitik*, 137–140

Specht-Riemenschneider, L. (2022c). Der Entwurf des Data Act: Eine Analyse der vorgesehenen Datenzugangsansprüche im Verhältnis B2B, B2C und B2G. *MMR Zeitschrift für IT-Recht und Recht der Digitalisierung*, 809–826

Storr, C. & Storr, P. (2017). Internet of Things: Rights to Data from a European Perspective. In M. Corrales et al. (Eds.), *New Technology, Big Data and the Law* (pp. 65–96) Springer Nature

Thaler v Commissioner of Patents [2021] FCA 879

The European Commission. (2022, February 23). *Proposal for a Regulation of the European Parliament and of the Council on harmonised rules on fair access to and use of data (Data Act)*. COM(2022) 68 final. Retrieved December 12, 2023, from https://eur-lex.europa.eu/legal-content/EN/TXT/PDF/?uri=CELEX:52022PC0068

The European Commission. (2022, February 23). *Commission Staff Working Document, Impact Assessment Report accompanying the document Proposal for a Regulation of the European Parliament and of the Council on harmonised rules on fair access to and use of data (Data Act)*. SWD(2022) 34 final. Retrieved December 12, 2023, from https://digital-strategy.ec.europa.eu/en/library/impact-assessment-report-and-support-studies-accompanying-proposal-data-act

The European Commission. (2022, May 5). *Proposal for a Regulation of the European Parliament and of the Council on the European Health Data Space*. COM(2022) 197 final. Retrieved December 12, 2023, from https://eur-lex.europa.eu/resource.html?uri=cellar:dbfd8974-cb79-11ec-b6f4-01aa75ed71a1.0001.02/DOC_1&format=PDF

The European Parliament and the Council. (2023, November 15). Regulation of the European Parliament and of the Council on harmonised rules on fair access to and use of data and amending Regulation (EU) 2017/2394 and Directive (EU) 2020/1828 (Data Act). PE-CONS 49/23. Retrieved December 12, 2023, from https://eur-lex.europa.eu/legal-content/EN/TXT/PDF/?uri=CONSIL:PE_49_2023_INIT

United Nations Economic and Social Council (ECOSOC). (2001, June 27). The Impact of the Agreement on Trade-Related Aspects of Intellectual Property Rights on Human Rights. Un Doc E/CN.4/Sub.2/2001/13
United Nations Secretary-General's High-Level Panel on Digital Cooperation. (2019). *Report of the UN Secretary-General's High-Level Panel on Digital Cooperation: The Age of Digital Interdependence*. New York/Geneva: United Nations Publications
Thouvenin, F. and Tamò-Larrieux, A. (2021). Data Ownership and Data Access Rights: Meaningful Tools for Promoting the European Digital Single Market? In M. Burri (Ed.), *Big Data and Global Trade Law* (pp. 316–339) Cambridge University Press
Veil, W. (2022). Ende des Wilden Westens oder wirrer Wildwuchs? *ZGI Zeitschrift für das gesamte Informationsrecht*, 197–198
von Schönfeld, M. and Wehkamp, N. (2018). Big Data and Smart Grid. In T. Hoeren, & B. Kolany-Raiser (Eds.), *Big Data in Context: Legal, Social and Technological Insights* (pp. 93–106) Springer Nature

Legal Nature of NFTed Artwork: A Comparative Study

Jia Wang and Arianna Alpini

1 Introduction

The platform economy is the tendency for commerce to move increasingly towards digital platform business models. Platforms are underlying computer systems that can host services allowing consumers, entrepreneurs, businesses and the general public to connect, share resources or sell products. Blockchain technology can support immutable and trustless transactions in a distributed and disintermediated way among various users. The trustless environments that blockchains have created enable peer-to-peer (P2P) sending and receiving transactions, smart contract agreements, and more. On the blockchain platform, tokenisation is used to transform ownerships and rights of particular assets into a digital form.

J. Wang (✉)
Durham Law School, Durham University, Durham, UK
e-mail: jia.wang2@durham.ac.uk

A. Alpini
Department of Law, University of Macerata, Macerata, Italy
e-mail: arianna.alpini@unimc.it

N. Naim (ed.), *Developments in Intellectual Property Strategy*,
https://doi.org/10.1007/978-3-031-42576-9_3

Tokenisation in blockchain opens up multiple new possibilities for businesses and individuals. Non-fungible tokens (NFTs) are widely adopted by the token owner in the form of a record and hash codes that show ownership of the unique token associated with a particular digital asset. Transactions are executed on smart contracts, sequences of computer codes that automatically execute pre-established instructions. Each block has a set amount of storage capacity, and once it is filled, it is 'chained' to the previously filled block. Most NFTs exist on the Ethereum blockchain, with permanent digital records of all cryptocurrency transactions.

Blockchain technologies and platforms inspired the creation of 'crypto art', that is, to tokenise artwork digitally and trade the tokens on the platform. Crypto art is disruptive to the traditional market of artwork in many ways. First, it solves the chronic problem of the piracy of artworks. NFTs enable authors to have exclusive control of their works stored in unique blocks with a private key, thus re-creating 'digital scarcity' of the works. The transaction of NFTed artwork occurs within a more decentralised power structure (Storey 2022). Second, NFTs make fine art investment more accessible and democratic. On the one hand, it enables a smaller investment of a fraction of an artwork. On the other hand, artwork can also be directly accessible from mobile phones and laptops without requiring storage space or the use of special equipment, which thus allows trade to be conducted more seamlessly (Hashtag Investing 2022, Hamilton 2022). Third, it enables direct transactions between the rightsholder and consumer without involving middlemen such as curators, galleries and art dealers (Drobitko 2022). Lastly, transactions of NFTed artwork increase liquidity and allow for higher transparency of data. Blockchain transactions are often completed in milliseconds, reducing the waiting time when selling NFTed artwork and allowing artists to be paid more quickly, thus increasing liquidity (Storey 2022). Not only are NFTs generally sold and traded in full public view (Storey 2022), but each transaction can also be traced and followed, as each NFT and its blockchain entries contain proof of current and past ownership, and all transactions involved (Storey 2022).

While NFTs look promising in many respects in trading artworks on digital platforms, legal risks must be addressed to capture the benefits of

NFTs fully. When buying an art piece, one does not purchase its copyright, which would have to be transferred separately. According to international copyright law, to own a piece of artwork does not necessarily entail the subsequent right to display the work in a public place and collect copyright royalties paid for the use of the work. The right to display and receive royalties remains with the copyright holder.

In this chapter, we explore the legal nature of NFTed artwork. When purchasing an NFTed artwork, what rights and interests does the purchaser acquire? Is holding an NFTed work equivalent to holding a physical copy? The objectives of this chapter are, first, to contextualise the discussion against the background of the trade of artworks in a blockchain environment; second, to examine the most recent legislation and court decisions concerning NFTs and cryptocurrency; finally, to conduct a comparative study between the selected common law and civil law systems of their concept of assets and property in relation to NFTs.

We undertake a comparative approach to facilitate the understanding of how different jurisdictions view the legal nature of NFTs. We look at the Anglo-American countries, then turn to Europe and China as civil law jurisdictions. Traditionally, the two legal systems view property rights differently. A comparative study offers insight into whether the convergence of law applies to legal issues of global relevance in a digital environment. Furthermore, this chapter conducts a case study of the most recent court decisions concerning property and intellectual property issues. As the legislation could lag behind the speedy advancement of technologies, court decisions offer a more timely reflection of the judiciary's attitude to NFTs.

This chapter proceeds as follows. The first section introduces blockchain and NFTs as an application of blockchain technologies, particularly the tokenisation of artwork. The second section examines how artworks are traded in the mortar-and-brick era and the digital era. The third and fourth sections scrutinise the common law and civil law approaches towards NFTs and the NFTed artwork. The last section offers a comparative analysis of the different approaches and provides concluding remarks.

2 Blockchain and the Tokenisation of Artwork

2.1 The Blockchains: Private, Public and Consortium Chain

Blockchains have been developed into three types: private chain, public chain and consortium chain. Private chains operate under the control of certain individuals or organisations. This is done by setting up a permissioned network, restricting the individuals allowed to participate in the network and transactions (Jayachandran 2017). As participants must obtain an invitation to join the network, private chains can filter out illegal activities within a chain (Iredale 2021). Yet as there are fewer nodes within the chain, the entire chain may become more easily compromised, posing a potential security risk (Brown 2022). Having a unique hash is vital for maintaining security throughout the different blocks because there are concerns about hackers tampering with the blocks and changing the hashes.

In contrast to a private chain, public chains, such as Bitcoin and Ethereum, are openly accessible to all who can access the internet (Jayachandran 2017), who can also see the ledger and participate in the consensus process (Iredale 2021). This design enables participants in a public chain to have equal rights and boosts transparency (Iredale 2021). Yet it also comes with drawbacks. For instance, a high amount of computational power is necessary for a public chain to function, to maintain the distributed ledger at a large scale (Jayachandran 2017). It takes a relatively long time to verify each transaction compared to other chains.

A consortium chain is a permissioned ledger where information can only be shared among a small group of organisations (Crypto News 2021). It is formed by combining various private blockchains belonging to different groups, where each group forms a node on the chain as a stakeholder. While each group manages its own blockchain, the data within it can be accessed, shared and distributed among the other organisations in the consortium (Bybit Learn 2022). A consortium chain is created among organisations to facilitate cooperation among these groups (Banerjee

2022). As a result, consortium chains offer benefits such as efficiency in decision-making (Bybit Learn 2022). However, there are also challenges. For example, a unified framework of industry standards for consortium blockchains (Banerjee 2022) urgently needs to be developed.

2.2 The Tokens: Fungible and Non-fungible

An NFT is a piece of digital artefact that represents the ownership of real-world assets. The influential NFT marketplaces in 2022 are OpenSea, Rarible, NBA Top Shot, Binance and Nifty Gateway, with most of them utilising cryptocurrencies as their payment method (Rodeck 2022). Whilst NFTs operate as a type of cryptocurrency (Fairfield 2021), it is vital to distinguish Bitcoin's and NFT's different natures. Bitcoins are interchangeable and indistinguishable, making them fungible tokens (Nakamoto 2019), while NFT is non-fungible because the associated data has a unique "hash value", a "unique and reproducible alphanumeric value from a specific data set" (Tipotsch 2021) derived from the artwork. There are different types of tokens. For example, using the ERC 20 Protocol, parties may create fungible tokens; using ERC 721 Protocol, they may create non-fungible tokens; using ERC 1238 Protocol, they may create non-transferable tokens (titles or badges).

There are three ways to create and issue tokens. The first method is through an Initial Coin Offering (ICO). This is a method of raising capital for new ventures (Delivorias 2021). The tokens can be exchanged for future products and services or confer a right to a share in future profits on holders (Knowledge at Wharton 2019). The tokens are then launched, and the business can use the proceeds to launch new products and services (CFI 2022). The second method is mining, where groups or individuals compete to solve complex mathematical problems (Trading Education 2021). The first one who solves the equation and validates the accuracy of a transaction in a block wins a reward (Trading Education 2021). Upon mining, tokens can be minted, that is, published on the blockchain and made available for purchase (Craig 2021). This can be done on platforms such as OpenSea, which allows one to mint tokens on the Ethereum blockchain by setting up a crypto wallet, creating a collection and uploading work (OpenSea Learn 2022). The third method to create tokens is through tokenisation by linking or embedding the economic value and the rights derived from the asset to digital tokens created on the blockchain (OECD 2020). The tokenised asset can then be listed and sold on NFT marketplaces. In this chapter, we mainly focus on the third tokenisation method for discussing NFTed artworks.

3 The Trading of Artworks

In the past, artworks were traded by transferring the physical object or licensing the use of the work without the transfer of ownership. Collective copyright licensing is managed by collective societies in Europe and China while in common law jurisdictions, by corporations specialising in collective copyright management. A common problem of collective copyright management is the high agency cost. Moreover, tracing and tracking the author of orphan works is less efficient due to the need for more technology. The intermediary, that is, the collective society, is confined by its structural and technological limits and cannot assist the rightsholder in fully capturing the value of artworks.

In the digital era, various data management tools help improve the efficiency of collective management. However, the agency cost and source-tracing problems still exist, although to a lesser extent. With the onslaught of blockchain and NFTs, it is time to revisit the agent-based transaction model. Do artists need an intermediary to manage their copyright if they can manage their own copyrighted works with secured NFTs and supporting platforms?

Although blockchain technologies seem to offer an ideally distributed and democratic digital world without intermediaries involving transaction costs (Drobitko 2022), in the new reality of business, NFTed artwork trading platforms emerge as new intermediaries. In China, the platforms can be divided into three categories. The first type comprises platforms that offer blockchain technology. Examples in China include Zhixin Chain, a platform based on Hyperledger technology, which is employed to execute smart contracts, digitise company chops and delineate ownership of intellectual property. Beyond China, Hyperledger

Fabric, hosted by the Linux Foundation, offers enterprise-grade blockchain technology for leaders in finance, banking and supply chains.

The second type is the platforms that support the trade of NFTed work. These may include platforms that facilitate the collection and resale of NFTed work, such as Netease Chain, a public chain which allows trade in a large variety of NFTed work, such as animation, music and 3-D models. Similarly, some provide the space for users to sell their NFTed products, for instance, the Two-Mirror Museum (双镜博物), a public chain that sells NFTed products related to culture, such as a digital collectible featuring the Palace Museum's only existing set of wedding garments belonging to a Qing dynasty empress. Such platforms can also be found outside China, for instance, Nifty Gateway, which cooperates with musicians and artists to create limited edition NFTs that are exclusively available on their platform.

The third type relates to those platforms that issue NFTed work. An example of such a platform is BlueFocus, a multinational company specialising in marketing and brand management services in media and design. Another example is CrowdCreate, whose services include assistance in crypto community management and crypto token marketing.

The increasingly involved artificial intelligence in creating artwork brings another dimension to the legal compliance for the trading of artworks. Unlike traditional artworks like painting, photography and music, which are protected by copyright, AI-created art is less concerned with copyright. AI-created art is also called generative art. Many NFT projects, such as CryptoPunks, Bored Ape Yacht Club, World of Women, Azuki, Chromie Squiggles, Clone X, and Moonbirds, involve generative art in the creation process. Generative art is generated wholly or in part by the algorithm and not in direct control of the programmer, who is an artist or commissioned by a customer. The programmer creates a programme consisting of one or more algorithms that randomly generate an artwork based on randomised parameter selections or by one or more inputs that are driven or operated to suggest a direction for the artwork. In more complex projects, artificial intelligence is programmed to make decisions during the entire process of creating an artwork (Dornis 2021). Different from the purchase of traditional artworks, the purchase of generative artwork is obtained upon the creation of the art, which coincides with the act of minting. The purchase of the NFTed AI-created artwork takes place by creating and minting the artwork.

However, NFTs are not the artwork, nor does it become the artwork. The NFT records the existence and ownership of the artwork onto the blockchain, and because no two NFTs are the same, and no two blockchain registrations can be the same, the tokenised asset linked to the NFT also can be considered unique and non-fungible. Each NFT contains metadata that describes the corresponding assets in order to prove the physical object's authenticity or rarity. The NFT represents the physical object in code written into the blockchain containing various information. This information frequently contains the name of the creator of the NFT, a URL linking to a representation of the underlying work of the NFT, the date it was minted, and any contractual terms that follow the NFT after it is sold. While the separate URL embedded in the NFT contains a link to a copy of the underlying work, it is not itself a copy of that work. Thus, an NFT is not a reproduction of content; it is merely a token that authenticates the source of the content. For this reason, NFTs themselves are not "copies" and thus not subject to copyright infringement. The metadata does not contain any recognisable content of the underlying work, nor does it describe its contents. Similarly, the metadata does not add, transform, or recast any underlying work.

Nevertheless, NFT establishes an exclusive ownership relationship with the underlying artwork. The hash is stored on a blockchain with an associated time stamp. Consequently, NFT keeps track of hash sales, so it is possible to trace the hand steps of the hash to the creator. This mechanism provides proof of authenticity and, simultaneously, ownership of the work. The transfer of an NFT connected to a work of art transfers the digital ownership of the authentic copy of the work; however, the purposes that can be pursued with this tool are different, so it is necessary to identify the crypto activity, the specific utility that the NFT is intended to create from time to time.

Authors can create and sell NFTs representing their works. In practice, the NFT digital art market recognises the owner of a "legitimate" NFTed work as the "owner" of the work, even though NFTs do not convey copyright ownership of the work (Frye 2022). NFT owners encourage others to use their work because popularity increases the value of the work.

Increasing the author's impact creates more value than controlling the use of the work. If the profit from selling NFTs alone is large enough to motivate authors, copyright is no longer necessary as a legal monopoly to reward authors. The value of art has always come from the reputation of the author and the scarcity of the work through "authenticity".

4 Legal Status of NFT: The Common Law Approaches

The premise of this property syllogism is that "a particular type of right (such as a chose in action, an intellectual property right or a beneficial interest under a trust) is the same type of right as a right to a tangible asset and must therefore be protected in the same way." (McFarlane and Douglas 2022, page 162). With this background in mind, it is perhaps unsurprising that crypto assets have been more readily accommodated within common law systems' vague notions of property than those of civilian systems.

The courts in England and Wales (English and Welsh cases), Singapore (Singaporean cases), and New Zealand (Ruscoe v Cryptopia Ltd. (in Liq) [2020]) have acknowledged bitcoins and other crypto assets as property within the common law. Property in the case law to date refers more to assets than things (Low and Hara 2022). This was also the advice of the LawTech Delivery Panel's UK Jurisdiction Taskforce in its Legal Statement on Cryptoassets and Smart Contracts. The key question is how crypto assets as property would fit within the common law's classificatory scheme for property. Unlike the civilian classification between movables and immovables, the common law classifies property into real and personal, with the former comprising mostly land. Personality is, in turn, classified into either choses in possession or choses in action.

4.1 The United Kingdom

The point on whether cryptocurrency could be a form of property was more fully developed in AA v Persons Unknown [2019] ("AA"). Bryan J noted that the immediate difficulty was that "English law traditionally views property as being of only two kinds, choses in possession and choses in action" (AA at [55], citing Colonial Bank v Whinney [1885] ("Colonial Bank")). Bitcoins, and other cryptocurrencies, did not fall neatly into either category and thus could not be classified as a form of property (AA at [56] and [58]). Bryan J, however, considered that it was "fallacious to proceed on the basis that the English law of property recognises no forms of property other than choses in possession and choses in action" (AA at [58]). In doing so, he cited extensively from the legal statement on crypto assets and smart contracts published by the UK Jurisdiction Task Force (the "Legal Statement"). Thus, the Task Force believed that Colonial Bank was not to be treated as limiting the scope of what kinds of things could be property in law. Rather, it showed the ability of the common law to stretch "traditional definitions and concepts to adapt to new business practices" (Legal Statement at [77]). The Legal Statement, therefore, formed the basis for Bryan J's conclusion that while a crypto asset might not be a thing in action based on a narrow definition of that term, it could still be considered property (AA at [59]). He made a finding that crypto assets such as Bitcoin were property, given that they met the four criteria set out in National Provincial Bank Ltd. v Ainsworth [1965] ("Ainsworth") at 1248 – namely that it must be "definable, identifiable by third parties, capable in its nature of assumption by third parties, and have some degree of permanence or stability".

The UK's High Court recently ruled that NFTs are property, and thus victims of NFT theft can now have their stolen assets frozen through court injunctions. The decision comes after months of repeated NFT thefts, as savvy hackers have exploited loopholes and poor security literacy to seize high-profile NFTs. In an earlier case involving NFTs (Osbourne v Persons Unknown [2022]), the court also found a claimant has a good arguable case that misappropriated crypto assets are held on a constructive trust is therefore clear that the courts are open to constructive trust claims as regards crypto assets. However, Ms. Osbourne did not go so far as to seek, as Mr. D'Aloia has, to ask the courts to consider a claim in which – in addition to the alleged fraudsters - the exchanges are also said to hold the crypto assets on constructive trust. In D'Aloia case, therefore, appears to be the first in which the Court has found that there is a good arguable case for this claim against the exchanges themselves.

D'Aloia case allows victims to obtain court injunctions against individuals whose crypto wallet has been identified as carrying a stolen NFT and to the NFT platform on which the stolen asset is being sold.

This ruling demonstrates that the English courts are open to entertaining constructive trust claims concerning crypto assets, not only against the fraudsters themselves but also against third-party exchanges. The possibility of such a claim has been lent further support by the Law Commission's analysis in their Consultation Paper on Digital Assets, published on 28 July 2022 (see paragraph 19.51). This would give victims of crypto-asset fraud a means of direct action against exchanges for breach of trust should they fail to comply with their duties as constructive trustees, having been notified that they are in the possession of fraudulently misappropriated crypto assets.

4.2 Singapore

In an earlier case of CLM v CLN [2022] SGHC 46 ("CLM"), Lee Seiu Kin J dealt with the question of whether stolen cryptocurrency assets, specifically Bitcoin and Ethereum, could be the subject of a proprietary injunction. Having considered the cases and the analysis in Ruscoe v Cryptopia Ltd. (in liq) [2020] ("Ruscoe"), the judge was of the view (at [46]) that the claimant, in that case, was able to prove an arguable case that the stolen cryptocurrency assets were capable of giving rise to proprietary rights, which could be protected via a proprietary injunction.

In Janesh s/o Rajkumar v Unknown Person [2022], the court noted that although NFTs have been characterised as certificates of ownership "powered by smart contracts and protected by blockchain technology" (Aksoy and Üner 2021, page 1115), NFTs represent an "ownership of a digital certificate of authenticity of commonly available digital art" (Low and Hara 2022). Nevertheless, the court disagrees with the 'NFT is certificate' approach. The court points out that NFTs are not just mere information but rather data encoded in a certain manner and securely stored on the blockchain ledger. (Janesh s/o Rajkumar v Unknown Person 2022, paragraph 58) Rather, NFTs provide instructions to the computer under a system whereby the "owner" of the NFT has exclusive control over its transfer from his wallet to any other wallet.

Lee Seiu Kin J adopted the Ainsworth test and upheld the following findings. First, an NFT with its unique metadata is definable (Janesh s/o Rajkumar, [44]). NFTs are not just mere information, but rather, data encoded in a certain manner and securely stored on the blockchain ledger (Janesh s/o Rajkumar, [58]) 'It provides instructions to the computer under a system whereby the "owner" of the NFT has exclusive control over its transfer from his wallet to any other wallet.' (Janesh s/o Rajkumar, [58]) Second, per the second requirement that the "asset must have an owner being capable of being recognised as such by third parties" (CLM, [45(b)], citing Ruscoe at [109]) the presumptive NFT owner would be whoever controls the wallet which is linked to the NFT an NFT with its private keys would be an asset, with an owner being capable of being recognised as such by third parties. The third requirement is that "that the right must be capable of assumption by third parties, which in turn involves two aspects: that third parties must respect the rights of the owner in that asset, and that the asset must be potentially desirable" The 'nature of the blockchain technology gives the owner the exclusive ability to transfer the NFT to another party, which underscores the "right" of the owner.' Lastly, an NFT has a relevant degree of permanence and stability as money in bank accounts which, nowadays, exist mainly in the form of ledger entries and not cold hard cash.

In summary, Singapore's first court decision on NFTs rejects the analogy between a title deed and a certificate of property. The court applies the Ainsworth criteria and upholds NFTs as property.

5 Legal Status of NFT: The Civil Law Approaches

5.1 The Theoretical and Legislative Discussion

Scholars pointed out that digital tokens may be considered "digital assets". The same approach is taken by the Gesetz über Token und VT-Dienstleister of Liechtenstein, which regulates tokens as assets (Vermögen, art. 4) (Teruel 2021). In fact, it has been stated that "all-European-legal systems of the member states regard not only corporeal thing as the objects of real rights but also incorporeal assets, such as patrimonial rights" (Von Bar and Drobnig 2004). However, some legal systems take a narrower approach concerning the scope of the property, which is limited to "corporeal things", as is the case under both German and Swiss law (e.g. §§90 Bürgerliches Gesetzbuch30 -BGB- or §641 Swiss Civil Code 31). This means that tokens could not be regarded as the object of property in these legal systems, e.g. in Germany, tokens have been defined as "eine faktische Vermögensposition", meaning 'a factual situation' (Lehman and Krysa 2019). Other EU legal systems have either incorporated a broader definition of the concept of a "thing" to include "patrimonial or valuable rights" (e.g. arts. 334.10 CC; §§292, 298 and 299 Allgemeines bürgerliches Gesetzbuch, ABGB35) or a broader definition of the concept of an "asset" (art. 3.1 Burgerlijk Wetboek -BW-), which makes regulating tokens as an object of ownership more accessible. For example, in Spain, the judgment of the Supreme Court 20/06/201937 denied the recognition of bitcoin as a legal tender (money) but considered it an "incorporeal asset". In Italy, tokens have been regarded as "digital assets" under the provisions of art. 810 Italian Civil Code ("Sono beni le cose che possono formare oggetto di diritti"); and art. 65 French Loi n. 486 categorises tokens as "incorporeal assets" (bien incorporel).

From an EU perspective, the Proposal for a Regulation of the European Parliament and of the Council on Markets in Crypto-assets (MiCA) 24 September 2020 aims to enhance legal certainty to crypto-assets while encouraging innovation and protecting consumers. However, this proposal does not cover the legal nature, the legal effects and the admissibility of using asset-backed tokens to transfer property rights. Tokens issued in blocks of fewer than 150 tokens are excluded from the Regulation. So, the Regulation does not cover small issuances, which are typically the case in the tokenisation of real-world assets. The European Union Court of Justice has ruled that cryptocurrencies fall into legal goods exempt from VAT (EUCG, sez. V, 22 October 2015, case - 214/2016).

China's first Civil Code became effective in 2021 and includes provisions peripherally relevant to virtual assets. In Book I General Provisions, Article 114 provides that civil subjects enjoy property rights (rights in rem), which are the exclusive rights to directly dominate a particular thing, including ownership, usufructuary rights, and security interests.

Article 116 is a Numerus Clausus that limits the types and contents of property rights exclusively by law. Article 127 provides that the Civil Code shall recognise the existing legal provisions for virtual property.

5.2 European Cases

Italian Supreme Court indicated that an equivalent function approach could be taken to allow the court to treat NFTs similarly to cryptocurrency with similar qualities. It held that the legal qualities of bitcoins depend on the purpose of the usage of the currency and the utility they produce. If a virtual currency is used for speculative purposes, it will be considered a financial product (security token). The Court identifies the requirements to qualify the securities offered (in the specific case LWF Coin) as financial instruments. The test includes the purpose of the use of capital, the expectation of return, and the risk directly linked to the use of capital. (Court of Cassation, Penal Section, 30 November 2021, n. 44337 and 22 November 2022, n. 44378).

The Court of Rome, IP Chamber (Docket No. 32072/2022) enjoined Blockeras s.r.l. from any production, marketing, promotion and offering for sale, directly and/or indirectly, in any way and form, of the NFTs and digital contents and ordered the defendant to withdraw from the market and remove from every website the NFTs and the digital contents associated or products in general covered by the injunction (Rome, 19 July 2022). The dispute concerned trademark infringement and unfair competition practice, consisting of the unauthorised use of words or figurative marks through the production, marketing and online promotion of digital playing cards with images that reproduced footballers' NFTs. The distinctive signs in question show the image of former player Christian (Bobo) Vieri wearing the Juventus shirt and the team's name. The Court did not express an opinion about the legal nature of NFT. Still, it stated that the circumstance that Bobo Vieri played for Juventus and that he granted permission to the use of his image through the creation of cards reproducing the player with the different shirts of the teams in which he played does not, therefore, exclude the need to request authorisation for using the registered trademarks owned by the teams whose shirts and names are reproduced. The decision indicated that the court viewed the infringement of IP by NFTs as equivalent to an infringement made through physical reproduction. Therefore, we can deduce that the court considers NFT as equivalent to (intellectual) property.

At the European level, the Court of Rome is the first to order an injunction to the creation and marketing of NFTs infringing registered trademarks. It also ordered the NFTs to be removed from the trading website. The decision represents a reference point at a global level at a time when strong attention is paid, by all operators in the sector, to the legal aspects of this new digital tool. It goes from who defines NFT as "a digital not interchangeable good, such as a photograph, a song or a video, whose property has been authenticated and stored in a database called blockchain and which can be collected, sold and exchanged on various online platforms" (Trevisi et al. 2022) to those who consider them as "unique digital certificates, registered in a blockchain, used as a means to register the ownership of an object, as a digital artwork or a collectible object" (EUIPO 2022). The decision represents an implicit accreditation of the interpretation - already adopted by the main national and international offices, including EUIPO, for which Class 9 is the one for registered trademarks used to distinguish certain types of "digital goods".

The Italian Court reiterates the provision of art. 97 of the Copyright Law, relating to the permitted uses of the right to the image of a person, does not extend to the use of trademarks possibly represented in the same image. The same consideration, however, also introduces the probably most important concept of the decision, which confirms the fact that the creation of NFTs - which are "goods intended for commercial sale" - requires specific authorisation from the proprietor of the trade mark, of which it, therefore, constitutes a separate infringement and distinct from the infringement constituted by the use of the trademark in the digital images associated with the NFT.

This confirms the preference for a legal definition of NFT that undertakes a dichotomy between the certificate and the content (Janesh s/o Rajkumar v Unknown Person 2022 SGHC 264). Above all, it explains the ratio of the same precautionary order, which is not by chance kept well distinguished between NFTs and the corresponding digital content, inhibits the "production, marketing, promotion and offer for sale, direct and/or indirect, in any way and form" of, on the one hand "of the NFT (non-fungible token)" and, on the other hand, of any other "digital content or product generally bearing the photograph, even modified, and/or the Juventus trademarks, as well as the use of said trademarks in any form and manner". This judgement echoes the US court decision involving Maison Hermes against the artist Mason Rothschild and Nike in relevant goods traded in StockX, a second-hand market.

This dichotomy of NFT/digital content cannot be ignored in the latter case. The judge needs to decide whether the creation of an NFT generates an intrinsic value rather than a mere digital certificate of ownership of the associated property, which, hypothetically, the person who mints and uploads the NFTed work is the legitimate owner of the work. We can deduce that even if someone possesses a good legitimately, it can be unlawful for the legitimate owner to produce NFTs of the good protected by IP rights. Since the judgments are still at a first summary level, we can only speculate on this issue.

The Commercial Law Court of Barcelona (Visual Entidad De Gestion De Artistas Plasticos/ Punto Fa, S.L. [2022] AJM B 1900/2022 – ECLI:ES: JMB: 2022:1900, Juzgado de lo Mercantil n° 09 de Barcelona) delivered one of the first judgments dealing with the relationship between intellectual property and NFT. The decision involves the fast fashion brand Mango and the Spanish collective society for artists VEGAP (Visual Entidad de Gestión de Artistas Plásticos). In March 2022, Mango exhibited a series of artworks created by Farkas, an artist, in a virtual museum on the Decentraland, a Web 3.0 site. Mango legitimately owns the original copy of the works. The collection was designed to reinterpret rather than directly reproduce the artworks, which are under copyright protection. VEGAP sued Mango for copyright infringement, arguing that the minting and displaying of the artworks infringed copyright; Mango argued that the NFTs were just a list on OpenSea and did not represent any proprietary rights per se. The Court ordered tokens to be de-listed, and further pointed out that the withdrawal of a work does not amount to destroying tokens since tokens can be used during the process. For this reason, the Court orders the claimant to provide a cryptocurrency wallet, with a deposit of EUR 1000 that will be used to maintain legal custody of the NFTs and orders OpenSea to transfer custody of those tokens to be deposited to the applicant's portfolio.

The first aspect of the dispute is the extent of Mango's rights as owner of the physical artwork. The ruling states that VEGAP transferred the right to display physical works publicly but nothing else. The Court assumes that the right to display does not give the right to digitise the work, display and sell it as NFT. The second question that the Court will have to examine is whether adapting a work in this way infringes copyright. Styles and ideas are not protected; only the expression of the idea is protected. If the Court decides that these designs are indeed in violation of relevant IP rights, the question is whether the minting NFT of a work without authorisation is unlawful in itself and whether the display and sale of such an NFT is a communication o the work to the public. It can be argued that an NFT may include a link to a copy of the work but not the work itself. The connection could not even be permanent and may be interrupted. In addition, the actual connection to work is not always easy to reach. If the link is to an IPFS file, it is not accessible unless a specialised browser like Brave, which can read IPFS links, is used. From this perspective, it is difficult to admit that "the act of minting" is protected as an exclusive right of the author.

5.3 Chinese Cases

In the first NFT court decision in China (Qice Technology Ltd. v A Technology Ltd), the Hangzhou Internet Court, an intermediate-level court, holds an NFT-trading platform liable for copyright infringement for an NFTed unauthorised reproduction of an artwork uploaded by its user. The court discusses similar issues regarding the nature of NFTs. It holds that the metadata exclusively and uniquely represents an artwork copy. It is identifiable by third parties and maintains the scarcity of the work in a digital form. Therefore, an NFTed work is a 'digital commodity', and NFTed copies of the work are digital assets. The trade of an NFTed work is essentially a transfer of ownership of the copy being tokenised and uploaded (page 18). Acquiring such an NFTed work entails obtaining the property rights and interests in that copy. It entails no license to use such digital assets nor a license or a transfer of the intellectual property rights of the underlying artwork (unless the sales agreement provides otherwise). In the further analysis of copyright infringement, the court distinguishes NFTed work from a physical object. It holds that the distribution right does not apply in this case because it only concerns the distribution of physical objects. The legitimate creator of an NFT should not be the person who possesses a copy of the underlying work but the person who owns the copyright or obtains a due license for the underlying work. Hence, it holds that the uploading of the NFTed work infringed on the right to disseminate work by information networks.

However, as the court is only a district-level court, it remains to be seen whether its ruling will be widely followed or is likely to be challenged in subsequent cases by other courts in China. In any case, as the authorities have not yet enacted any formal NFT laws or regulations, the court's insights in the judgment are meaningful, and NFT players in China should carefully consider the implications of the ruling.

6 Conclusions

The value of art has always come from the reputation of the author and the scarcity of the work through 'authenticity'. NFTs offer artists the opportunity to secure incomes with tracing and tracking functions and embedded smart contracts while encouraging the dissemination of artwork that cannot be reproduced without authorisation. If the profit from selling NFTs is large enough to motivate authors, copyright as a legal monopoly is no longer necessary to generate rewards. Recognising NFTs as property encourages artists to be open to the market, which helps create cultural prosperity and increase social welfare.

The NFT is more than a recording of digital work. Minting an NFTed work is to record the work on the blockchain through an identification code. The creation of the digital tokenised work (i.e. registered blockchain with hash code) involves the acquisition of ownership by the registration holder. NFTed artwork might evoke the question of exclusive possession and control of the work, including property and IP rights. The right to tokenise a work protected by copyright belongs to the owner of the copyright or those who have the authorisation of the owner; beyond this hypothesis, this right belongs to the owner of NFTed work. Consequently, it is necessary to distinguish NFTs from NFTed artwork. The NFT is a mechanism for forming the ownership of a right of use and disposition of digital work in the hands of the person who registers the NFTs.

Although the judiciary from different jurisdictions has been willing to extend the protection for brick-and-mortar property to NFTed artworks, NFTs are at the risk of misrepresenting or even infringing IP rights in a work minted into NFTs. Possessing an NFT does not necessarily confer any legal right over the digital or physical object the NFT refers to. Several proposals have been advanced to overcome this limitation to the concept of NFT. Some try to strike a balance between the legal and the technical dimension, incorporating aspects of copyright law into the metadata of the NFT or in accompanying documentation; others propose to incorporate the actual work into the underlying smart contract. While many commentators are critical at this point (Ryan 2021), others, like Fairfield, see the potential of NFTs as forms of 'unique digital property', re-establishing personal property rights that have been lost to user agreements and other instruments of uneven bargaining power (Fairfield 2021).

In the UK, the Task Force took the view that Colonial Bank was not to be treated as limiting the scope of what kinds of things could be property in law. Instead, it showed the ability of the common law to stretch "traditional definitions and concepts to adapt to new business practices". National Provincial Bank Ltd. v Ainsworth [1965] has established a four-factored test for the property as something "definable, identifiable by third parties, capable in its nature of assumption by third parties, and have some degree of permanence or stability". In Singapore, the court rejected the analogy between a title deed for real property and NFTs as a certificate for digital assets. Rather, it adopted the Ainsworth criteria and upheld NFTs as property.

In Europe, although some jurisdictions traditionally take a narrow approach concerning the scope of the property, which is limited to "corporeal things", many others are more open to including incorporeal assets, such as patrimonial rights, into real rights. The court decisions discussed in Sect. 5 demonstrate that cryptocurrency and NFTs are considered digital assets (Calzolaio 2020). The Italian and Spanish Courts noted that NFTs, on the one hand, bear a certifying function and, on the other hand, link to specific content. China's first Civil Code explicitly recognises virtual property as an object protectable by law. In the first NFT-concerned case, the court distinguishes the NFTed work from a physical object and holds that an NFTed work is a 'digital commodity', and NFTed copies of the work are digital assets. It adopts a test similar to the Ainsworth test that evaluates whether the data is unique and securely linked to a work and is identifiable by third parties. It is consensus that while the right of the owner to mint and tokenise a work is to be fully protected, it cannot be overlooked that this right must be exercised in compliance with the principle of economic solidarity and fair competition.

The comparison between the legal systems implies an increasing level of convergence of law towards a harmonised concept of digital assets in a world built on blockchain and tokens. In comparing the common law and civil law systems, convergence of law is emerging in the digital world. The legal systems have advanced closer towards a concept of property with many shared features. First, the data must be stored securely on the blockchain ledger. The nature of blockchain technology gives the owner the exclusive ability to transfer the NFT to another party, which underscores the "right" of the owner. Second, the data should be capable of being recognised by third parties. Third, the data has intrinsic value that is respected and potentially desirable by third parties. Lastly, an NFT has a relevant degree of permanence and stability as money in bank accounts which, nowadays, exist mainly in the form of ledger entries and not cold hard cash. Property is moving from a static concept to a concept of act and activity. At the same time, ownership is the link between the owner and the worthy interest to be realised and guaranteed.

NFTed artworks are considered incorporeal assets that confer quasi-property rights and interests. The legal principle of numerus clausus is an instrument for legal certainty. However, reality goes beyond the dogmas of the legal tradition. The jurist must take an evolutionary leap forward to adapt the mechanisms and techniques of law to emerging digital technologies that change the societal ecosystem. The concept of property per se and the rights deriving from the property need a recalibration that shifts from focusing on exclusive control to the use of the thing.

Attention must be paid to the consideration that the "thing" becomes a juridical good as a reference point and content of legal situations if it has a socially appreciable utility and finds in the orderly system an evaluation in terms of merit (Perlingieri 1990). The artificial exclusivity – created by the relationship between the account/portfolio and the hash via NFT – that represents the copy of the underlying value – evokes the proprietary logic even if its dynamics undermine any theoretical definition for the benefit of the valuation of the interests involved.

References

Articles

Aksoy, P. C. & Üner, Z. (2021). NFTs and Copyright: Challenges and Opportunities. Journal of Intellectual Property Law & Practice, 16(10), 1115–1126.

Bybit Learn (2022). 'Consortium blockchain', available at https://learn.bybit.com/glossary/definition-consortiumblockchain/, accessed on 20 September 2023.

Calzolaio, E. (2020). Il bitcoin come oggetto di property. Note a margine di una recente sentenza della High Court. Il Foro Italiano, CXLV 10, 494–500.

De Caria, R. (2020). Blockchain and Smart Contracts. Italian Law Journal, 6(1), 363–380.

De Caria, R. (2018). The Legal Meaning of Smart Contracts. European Review of Private Law, 26(6), 731–752.

Dornis, T.W. (2021). Of 'Authorless Works' and 'Inventions without Inventor' – The Muddy Waters of 'AI Autonomy' in Intellectual Property Doctrine. European Intellectual Property Review, forthcoming 2021, 1–28

Fairfield, J. (2021). Tokenized: The Law of Non-Fungible Tokens and Unique Digital Property. Indiana Law Journal, forthcoming. https://ssrn.com/abstract=3821102

Frye, B. L. (2022). After Copyright: Pwning NFTs in a Clout Economy. The Colombia Journal of Law and Arts, 45(3), 341–353.

Lehman, M., & Krysa F. (2019). Blockchain, smart contracts und token aus der sicht des (internationale) privatrechts. Bonner Rechts Journal 2019 (Issue 2): 90–96.

Moringiello, J. M. & Odinet, C.K. (2022) The Property Law of Tokens. Florida Law Review, 74, 607–671. https://ssrn.com/abstract=3928901 or https://doi.org/10.2139/ssrn.3928901

Murray, M.D. (2022a). Generative and AI Authored Artworks and Copyright Law. Hastings Communications and Entertainment Law Journal, 45(1), 28–43. https://ssrn.com/abstract=4152484 or https://doi.org/10.2139/ssrn.4152484

Murray, M.D. (2022b). NFT Ownership and Copyrights. https://ssrn.com/abstract=4152468 or https://doi.org/10.2139/ssrn.4152468

Nakamoto, S. (2019). Bitcoin: A Peer-to-Peer Electronic Cash System, 'Bitcoin: A Peer-to-Peer Electronic Cash System', https://papers.ssrn.com/sol3/papers.cfm?abstract_id=3440802, accessed on 20 September 2023.

Perlingieri, P. (1990). L'informazione come bene giuridico. Rass. dir. Civ., 326–338.

Rodeck & Hooson. (2022). 'Top NFT Marketplaces of 2023', available at https://www.forbes.com/uk/advisor/investing/cryptocurrency/best-nft-marketplaces/, accessed on 20 September 2023.

Ryan, T. R. (2021, December 2). Will the Artworld's NFT Wars End in Utopia or Dystopia? Art Review. https://artreview.com/will-the-artworld-nft-wars-end-in-utopia-or-dystopia/.

Teruel, G.M.R., Simon-Moreno, H. (2021). The digital tokenization of property rights: a comparative perspective. Computer Law and Security Review, 41, 4–5.

Von Bar C., & Drobnig, U. (2004). 'The Interaction of Contract Law and Tort and Property Law in Europe: A Comparative Study', Sellier de Gruyter (2004). Study on property law and non-contractual law as they relate to contract law, European Commission–Health and Consumer Protection Directorate-General, Brussels, Belgium, available at: https://www.academia.edu/1131084/Study_on_property_law_and_noncontractual_law_as_they_relate_to_contract_law (last access: 7 November 2016).

Book Chapters

Low, K. F. K. & Hara, M. (2022). Cryptoassets and Property. In Sjef van Erp & Katja Zimmermann (eds), Edward Elgar Research Handbook on EU Property Law (forthcoming), available at SSRN: https://ssrn.com/abstract=4103870 or http://dx.doi.org/10.2139/ssrn.4103870

Cases

AA v Persons Unknown, [2019a] EWHC 3556 (Comm)
Colonial Bank v Whinney [1885] 30 Ch.D 261
CLM v CLN [2022] SGHC 46
Janesh s/o Rajkumar v Unknown Person [2022] SGHC 264
Juventus Football Club S.p.A. v Blockeras s.r.l. [2022a] Court of Rome, IP Chamber, Docket No.32072
National Provincial Bank Ltd v Ainsworth [1965] AC 1175
Osbourne v Persons Unknown & Anor [2022] EWHC 1021 (Comm) (10 March 2022)
Qice Technology Ltd v A Technology Ltd ([2022] Zhe 0192 Min Chu No. 1008
Ruscoe v Cryptopia Ltd (in Liq) [2020] NZHC 728, [2020] 2 NZLR 809
Skatteverket v Hedqvist [2015a] EUCG, sez. V, 22 October 2015, case - 264/2014
Visual Entidad De Gestíon De Artistas Plásticos v Punto Fa, S.L. [2022a] AJM B 1900/2022 - ECLI:ES: JMB: 2022:1900, Juzgado de lo Mercantil n° 09 de Barcelona

English and Welsh Cases

AA v Persons Unknown [2019b] EWHC 3556 (Comm)
Danisz v Persons Unknown [2022] EWHC 280 (QB) at [13]
Fetch.AI Ltd v Persons Unknown Category A [2021] EWHC 2254 (Comm) at [9]
Ion Science Ltd v Persons Unknown (unreported EWHC(Ch) 21 December 2020, Butcher J) at [11]
Mr Dollar Bill Ltd v Persons Unknown [2021] EWHC 2718 (Ch) at [10]
Shair.Com Global Digital Services Ltd v Arnold 2018 BCSC 1512 at [15]
Vorotyntseva v Money-4 Ltd [2018] EWHC 2596 (Ch) at [13]
Wang v Darby [2021] EWHC 3054 (Comm) at [55]

Singaporean Cases

B2C2 Ltd v Quione Pte Ltd [2019] SGHC(I) 03 [2019] 4 SLR 17 at [142], but the issue was left open on appeal: [2020] SGCA(I) 02, [2020] 2 SLR 20 at [144]. See now, however, CLM v CLN [2022] SGHC 46 at [46].

European Cases

Juventus Football Club S.p.A. v Blockeras s.r.l. [2022b] Court of Rome, IP Chamber, Docket No.32072

Skatteverket v Hedqvist [2015b] EUCG, sez. V, 22 October 2015, case - 264/2014

Visual Entidad De Gestíon De Artistas Plásticos v Punto Fa, S.L. [2022b] AJM B 1900/2022 - ECLI:ES: JMB: 2022:1900, Juzgado de lo Mercantil n° 09 de Barcelona

Others

Banerjee, A. (2022). Everything you need to know about consortium blockchain. Retrieved 4 November, 2022, from https://www.blockchain-council.org/blockchain/everything-you-need-to-know-about-consortium-blockchain/

Brown, E. (2022). Comparing public and private blockchain features, pros & cons. Retrieved 5 November, 2022, from https://bsvblockchain.org/news/comparing-public-and-private-blockchain-features-pros-cons

Bybit Learn (2022). Consortium blockchain. Retrieved 4 November, 2022, from https://learn.bybit.com/glossary/definition-consortium-blockchain/

CFI (2022a). Initial Coin Offering (ICO). Retrieved 6 November, 2022, from https://corporatefinanceinstitute.com/resources/cryptocurrency/initial-coin-offering-ico/

CFI (2022b). Minting Crypto. Retrieved 6 November, 2022, from https://corporatefinanceinstitute.com/resources/cryptocurrency/minting-crypto/

Craig, J. (2021). Crypto Minting vs Mining: What's the Difference? Retrieved 6 November, 2022, from https://phemex.com/blogs/crypto-minting-vs-crypto-mining

Crypto News (2021). What is Consortium Blockchain? Retrieved 4 November, 2002, from https://crypto.news/glossary/consortium-blockchain/

Delivorias, A. (2021). Understanding Initial Coin Offerings. European Parliamentary Research Services. Retrieved 6 November, 2022, from https://www.europarl.europa.eu/RegData/etudes/BRIE/2021/696167/EPRS_BRI(2021)696169_EN.pdf

Drobitko, A.(2022). Can Artists Still Benefit From NFTs? Retrieved 6 November 2022, from https://www.forbes.com/sites/forbesbusinesscouncil/2022/06/29/can-artists-still-benefit-from-nfts/?sh=57efba0a648d

EUIPO, EUIPO Draft Guidelines 2023 edition. Retrieved 13 January, 2023, from https://euipo.europa.eu/ohimportal/nl/draft-guidelines 2023

Hamilton, A. (2022). The Private and Public Benefits of NFT Art. Retrieved 6 November 2022, from https://www.zenofineart.com/blogs/news/the-private-and-public-benefits-of-nft-art

Hashtag Investing (2022). Top 6 Benefits Of NFT's For Artists And Reasons To Use Them In 2022. Retrieved 6 November, 2022, from https://www.hashtag-investing.com/blog/top-benefits-of-nfts-for-artists

Iredale, G. (2021). Public vs Private Blockchain: How do they differ? Retrieved 4 November, 2022, from https://101blockchains.com/public-vs-private-blockchain/

Jayachandran, P. (2017). The difference between public and private blockchain. Retrieved 4 November, 2022, from https://www.ibm.com/blogs/block-chain/2017/05/the-difference-between-public-and-private-blockchain/

Knowledge at Wharton (2019). How to Design an Effective Initial Coin Offering. Retrieved 6 November, 2022, from https://knowledge.wharton.upenn.edu/article/design-effective-initial-coin-offering/

McFarlane, B. and Douglas, S. (2022). Property, Analogy and Variety. Oxford Journal of Legal Studies, 42, 161–186.

OECD (2020). The Tokenisation of Assets and Potential Implications for Financial Markets. OECD Blockchain Policy Series. Retrieved 6 November, 2022, from https://www.oecd.org/finance/The-Tokenisation-of-Assets-and-Potential-Implications-for-Financial-Markets.pdf

OpenSea Learn (2022b). What is minting? Retrieved 6 November, 2022, from https://opensea.io/learn/what-is-minting-nft

Rarible (2022). How do I sell my NFT on Rarible? Retrieved 6 November, 2022, from https://rarible.com/how-it-works/using-rarible/how-do-i-sell-my-nft-on-rarible

Reiff, N. (2022). Decentralised Autonomous Organisation (DAO): Definition, Purpose and Example. Retrieved 5 November, 2022, from https://www.investopedia.com/tech/what-dao/

Storey, A. (2022). 11 Surprising Benefits of NFTs for Artists. Retrieved 6 November, 2022, from https://postergrind.com/11-surprising-benefits-of-nfts-for-artists

Tipotsch, A., Formulating a Smart Contract and Minting an NFT. Retrieved 13 January 2023, from https://www.schoenherr.eu/content/formulating-a-smart-contract-and-minting-an-nft/

Trading Education (2021). Cryptocurrency Mining Explained. Retrieved 6 November 2022, from https://trading-education.com/cryptocurrency-mining-explained

Trevisi, C., Visconti, R.M., Cesaretti, A. (2022). Non-Fungible Tokens (NFT): business models, legal aspects, and market valuation. Rivista di Diritto dei Media. Retrieved 13 January, 2023, from https://www.medialaws.eu/rivista/non-fungible-tokens-nft-business-models-legal-aspects-and-market-valuation/

Whittaker, M. (2022). How Does Bitcoin Mining Work? Retrieved 6 November 2022, from https://www.forbes.com/advisor/investing/cryptocurrency/bitcoin-mining/

Intellectual Property Regulation of Artificial Intelligence: A Matter of Time or a Step Too Far?

Lucius Klobucnik

1 Introduction

Artificial intelligence (AI) has been disrupting the world of technology and computing for many years, bringing significant benefits to our daily lives. Ever more sophisticated AI systems do not only supplement the work of humans, but can perform tasks which have been traditionally reserved exclusively for humans. AI can be subdivided into a weak (or narrow) AI and strong AI, according to whether it is designed to tackle single task or can accomplish tasks across multiple domains. AI has been increasingly involved in creative and inventive processes which result in assets qualifying for intellectual property protection, whether by copyright or patent law. However, intellectual property law was designed to protect inventions and creations of a human mind, thus seemingly leaving AI outside of the scope of protection. Currently, the prominence of AI has been set to shake up the foundations of intellectual property law

L. Klobucnik (✉)
Aston Law School, Aston University, Birmingham, West Midlands, UK
e-mail: l.klobucnik@aston.ac.uk

N. Naim (ed.), *Developments in Intellectual Property Strategy*,
https://doi.org/10.1007/978-3-031-42576-9_4

(IP) law. IP law was established in order to recognise the fruits of human ingenuity, creativity, and inventiveness. Indeed, for a long time, mankind assumed that only humans are capable of producing creative works or inventions. But what happens if the human element is taken away from the creative or inventive process? Can IP law accommodate the ingenuity of machines or will legislative changes be required? One of the widely discussed questions has been whether AI can generate inventions or copyright-protected works without human contribution. Suggestions have been provided by academics, governments, policy makers, international institutions (most notably the World Intellectual Property Organisation – WIPO), but legislators have been hesitant to reflect any of them into the existing legal framework. Policy discussions have been revolving around the question whether intellectual property law, especially copyright and patent law, ought to be revised to account for technological developments in AI. For instance, the European Parliament, in its resolution from February 2017 noted that ever more sophisticated AI requires the legislation in virtually every area to consider its legal and ethical implications without stifling innovation. In the UK, both copyright and patent law systems lack specific regulation regarding eligibility of robot generated works or robot inventions. The UK Government set out a goal to change this, by asking the public in Autumn 2021 whether the current rules on copyright and patent are sufficient to accommodate creations and inventions by AI, or whether a new set of rules is needed. A large variety of stakeholders exchanged their views with the UK Government. This may lead to new policy options and potential changes in law, which will be discussed here. This chapter does not aim to provide responses as to whether copyright and patent law is ripe for amendment. Rather, it aims to discuss involvement of AI in the IP value chain – not only with respect to AI as a creator/inventor (i. e. before IP protection arises), but also the role of AI as a user of IP protected assets. Challenges brought by AI are discussed here with respect to two areas of intellectual property – copyright and patents.

2 AI and Copyright

2.1 Originality of Works Created by AI

Perhaps the biggest challenge with respect to copyright-protected works created by AI lies in the question whether these works will be able to meet the central criterion for copyright protection – originality. This criterion may be hard to reconcile with AI-generated works. Especially the test of originality, established in the InfoPaq case and applicable in the UK and the EU, is based on the premise of an author's own intellectual creation, thus presupposing a human quality. The criterion of originality focuses on the interaction between the author and the work and has an inherently human element. The human authorship requirement raises questions with regard to AI creations. In particular, when robots start operating more independently, making their choices less predictable and foreseeable to either their users or their programmers. Human involvement in the process of creation becomes more difficult to identify. McCutcheon suggests that the criterion of originality would be applied on a hypothetical basis – if the work had been authored by a human, or if that human could be identified, would it be original? The test of originality is deeply rooted in copyright legislation and in case law. Copyright exceptions for the sake of AI-created works are currently not being considered.

Pursuant to the seminal InfoPaq decision, which plays a leading role in understanding the originality requirement, the Court of Justice of the European Union (CJEU) pointed in the direction that a creative output has to have a human input. Answering the question whether eleven words could enjoy copyright protection, the CJEU clarified that it was 'only through the choice, sequence and combination of those words that the author may express his creativity in an original manner and achieve a result which is an intellectual creation'. In defining the elements of originality, the CJEU did not look into the result of creativity but rather focused on the process of creation. The clear focus of the CJEU on the human element was confirmed in the case of Painer, where the CJEU explained that an intellectual creation was author's own if it reflected the author's personality. The process of creation of a copyright-protected work requires the author to make free and creative choices, which ultimately reflect the author's personal touch. Following these criteria, it seems difficult to detach a copyright protected work from a human element. Although the CJEU does not expressly refer to a human touch as an authorship requirement, it indicates quite clearly that some kind of a human quality has to be present in the creation process. According to Ramalho, where there is no human author, a work cannot be original, and without originality, a work cannot be protected by copyright.

The concept of originality underlines the need for a human author, insofar as personality can be described as a purely human attribute. With respect to the requirement concerning free and creative choices, Van Gompel argues that even though the autonomy of authors to make free choices is naturally restricted, as individual creators operate within social, technical and institutional environments, at least some of these choices are internal and self-imposed. The underlying rationale for free and creative choices seems to be that these choices are made consciously, i. e. by a conscious being. Moreover, if copyright protects expression of ideas, it would be questionable to think of an idea as being expressed by an AI machine.

The international legal framework for copyright, namely the Berne Convention, does not explicitly define authorship, nor does it explicitly require a human author. However, one of the prominent international copyright commentators, Sam Ricketson, argues that the Berne Convention is very 'anthropocentric', e. g. by granting moral rights to the author, by linking the duration of protection to the life of the author or by referring to 'intellectual creations'. The logical conclusion seems to be that attributing moral rights to an AI machine or to link copyright protection to the 'life' of a subject matter would not make sense. The view that copyright-protected works can only have a human author is corroborated by the International Association for the Protection of Intellectual Property (AIPPI), which argues that without human intervention, there should be no copyright protection of AI-generated works. Indeed, with its robust exclusive rights and a long term of protection, copyright may not be the most suitable vehicle for the protection of AI-generated works. However, the copyright law framework may offer a potential vehicle for protection of AI-generated works in the form of neighbouring rights (related rights) – with a shorter duration and without the element of moral rights, as opposed to copyright. A legislative construct that may serve as an example is already present in the UK copyright law – computer-generated works. Let us have a closer look at the relevance of the debate on computer-generated works for AI-generated works.

2.2 Potential Legislative Lead Given by Computer-Generated Works

One of the main questions related to AI and copyright is who is the author (and thus the owner) of AI-*generated works. In the United Kingdom, the Copyright, Designs and Patents Act (CDPA) 1988 already has a rather unique provision on the so-called computer-generated works (CGWs), which was added to the UK copyright law as a response to technological challenges, i. e. a (digitally) created work that seemingly has no author, or at least no human author. In case of CGWs, the author for the purposes of copyright law is the person by whom the arrangements necessary for the creation of the work are undertaken. When dealing with an 'artificial author', the UK opted for a legislative route where the natural person behind the computer rather than the actual maker (the computer itself) is to be considered an author for copyright law purposes. The difference between CGWs and other copyright-protected works is that in the case of the former, the human author does not benefit from moral rights and the term of protection is shorter (50 years from the end of the calendar year of the creation). Such a right resembles a neighbouring right rather than copyright in the sense of an author's right, although the CDPA does not use such a language. The legislative construction of CGWs leaves some questions on authorship open to interpretation. For instance, who is the person by whom the arrangements necessary for the creation of the work have to be undertaken – will it be the person overseeing the operation of the machine, or the person who provides the actual device, or the computer programmer who wrote the underlying code?

3 An Appropriate Mechanism to Use Copyright-Protected Works by AI

3.1 AI Creator Learning from Existing Copyright-Protected Works

The copyright law framework seems to suggest that a human element is indispensable in creation of copyright protected works. However, how do AI-generated works get created in the first place? It has to be noted that in order to come up with artistic outputs, AI systems first have to engage with already existing works. Put simply, AI has to be fed data (or works) to come up with a creation. Technically, AI is combining different works together to create a new work. Such a process poses a question as to whether the use of copyright-protected content for AI training purposes can be considered copyright infringement. Some copyright owners have already expressed their discontent with AI using their works for training purposes. Some of the biggest online picture repositories – GitHub and Getty Images – have opposite views on whether AI training amounts to infringement. While the former calls for an exception from copyright protection and suggests a contributor fund to remunerate authors, the latter decided not to offer AI-generated works on their platform at all. AI tools can generate works, which resemble particular art styles of concrete artists as a result of those works being fed into AI machine learning. These are the so-called 'text-to-image' AI systems – in the past, they have been available only to a select group of tech insiders. Recently, an image generated with an AI system called Midjourney won an art competition at the Colorado State Fair. In order for a machine to generate an image, it must be trained on large amount of metadata, which may include billions of images scraped from the internet, paired with written descriptions. On the one hand, copyright owners should be remunerated if their works are being used. On the other hand, it would be prohibitive to licence every single image in a dataset before using it. If we opt for the licensing way, machine learning may become impossible. The concept of fair dealing, known in UK law, may potentially be used for AI-generated content based on AI training. Recently, there have also been some suggestions by the UK Government to introduce a data-mining exception from copyright infringement for the purpose of AI-training. However, the legislator should carefully weigh for such an exception not to go so far as to suggest that artworks fed into AI systems can be used without the rights holder's consent. Let us have a closer look at the proposed exception and its potential legal implications.

3.2 Text and Data Mining (TDM) Exception

3.2.1 Text and Data Mining Exception Promoted by the UK Government

The UK Government had been planning to introduce a new copyright and database exception which allows text and data mining for any purpose, commercial or non-commercial. It has to be noted, however, that these plans have been halted due to a significant backlash from the creative industries. Therefore, the fate of the proposed text and data mining exception remains unclear and the UK is currently left with the exception only covering non-commercial research, which is generally more restrictive than in other jurisdictions around the world. In any case, the proposed text and data mining exception deserves our attention. Text and data mining (TDM) means using computational techniques to analyse large amounts of information to identify patterns, trends and other useful information. TDM is used for training AI systems in order to perform tasks in journalism, marketing, business analytics and by cultural institutions. TDM can be understood as a research technique to collect information from large amounts of digital data through automated software tools. In the process of TDM, the analysed material is first being identified and data is individually collected or organised in pre-existing databases. After that, substantial quantities of material are being copied. These materials are first turned into a machine-readable format compatible with a technology to be deployed for the TDM so that structured data can be extracted and pre-processed material is possibly uploaded on a platform, depending on a TDM technique to be deployed. Subsequently, data is being extracted and recombined to identify patterns into the final output.

It is worth recalling that the UK was the first country in Europe to have a TDM exception – limited text and data analysis exception was introduced in S. 29A CDPA taking advantage of the possibilities under Article 5(3)(a) of the InfoSoc Directive. The introduction of the TDM exception was essential to unlock the potential of the British research and unburden researchers from encumbrances and uncertainties. The current exception covers only non-commercial purposes. TDM usually requires copying of the material to be analysed. Therefore, in particular, the infringement of reproduction as an act restricted by copyright pursuant to the CDPA comes into question (section 17 CDPA). TDM techniques open up tensions between rights and freedoms of text and data miners on the one hand and exclusive rights of copyright holders on the other hand. The (potentially) new regime of TDM exceptions should be mindful of the balance of interests of these two groups. Reliance on the current exceptions to the reproduction right do not provide a sufficient certainty for TDM. Currently, exceptions to reproduction right based on S.29A CDPA only cover temporary, transient and incidental reproductions with no economic significance. Especially the last requirement is hard to satisfy. Thus, the risk of infringing copyright when performing TDM activities is relatively high. The intention of the proposed exception is that rights holders will no longer be able to charge for UK licences for TDM and will not be able to contract or opt out of the exception. The new provision may also affect those who have built partial business models around data licensing. The main safeguard for rights holders will be the requirement of lawful access. That means that rights holders could choose the platform where they make their works available, including charging for access via subscription or single charge. They will also be able to take measures to ensure the integrity and security of their systems.

3.2.2 TDM Exception Not Allowing Rights Holders to Opt Out

The UK Government intends that anyone with lawful access to material protected by copyright should be able to carry out this analysis without further permission from the copyright owner. Among other uses, data mining can be used when training AI systems. For example, machine-learning software which has been trained on large repositories of computer code is able to intelligently suggest new code to programmers. Although the government claims that the suggested TDM exception will bring benefits to a wide range of stakeholders in the UK, including researchers, AI developers, and cultural heritage institutions, the biggest concern of copyright holders may be that they will not be able to control who has access to their work. While the TDM exception may encourage innovation in AI technology and promote its use for the public good, it should also aim to preserve the central role of AI in promoting human creativity. Under the proposed TDM exception, rights holders will not be allowed to opt out of text and data mining AI systems. This proposal has already attracted some criticism. During the stakeholder response phase to the UK Government's AI and IP Consultation, music rights holders expressed their concerns that music would be reduced to mere data for the purposes of mining. The proposal does not seem to take into account that datasets are present in all types of works, not only in databases. It was argued that the non-existence of the opt out regime essentially removes any opportunity for creators to get compensation for their creativity and talent, and they will also not be able to prevent the abuse of their work by a computer. Some right holders stated their preference to remove their works from datasets used to train AI systems.

3.2.3 Potential New TDM regime

The proposed TDM regime should promote a balance between all stakeholders involved in the copyright value chain – rights holders, users, and consumers. TDM is not only important for non-commercial research, but also for other purposes, such as freedom of speech and journalism. Therefore, allowing access of a large variety of entities to TDM is essential. Most importantly, TDM is a tool for AI-enabled innovation. Much of the current and future development of AI depends on TDM. Therefore, it is important to ensure that no entities are excluded from a possibility to perform TDM activities. For instance, start-ups, which are not affiliated with any research institution and operate on a for-profit basis, cannot currently avail themselves of the TDM exception and can get caught up in robust licensing mechanisms which can prevent start-ups from emerging.

Researchers are faced with legal uncertainty as to whether and under which conditions can they carry out TDM on content they have lawful access to. TDM exceptions can and should go further in adapting to the digital environment. It has to be noted that the TDM exception is also dealt with in the EU Copyright in the Digital Single Market Directive 2019/ 790 (EU CDSM Directive). Unlike the current UK TDM exception, the TDM exception pursuant to the EU CDSM Directive applies to both commercial and non-commercial mining purposes. The difference between the two being that if mining is performed for non-commercial purposes (i. e. by research organisations or cultural institutions), right holders do not have a right to opt out of the TDM exception. If TDM is done for commercial purposes, right holders are allowed to opt out, i. e. to contractually override the exception to the reproduction right infringement. The currently applicable UK regime of TDM exceptions does not distinguish between mining for commercial or non-commercial purposes. The newly proposed TDM exception blurs the distinction between TDM done for commercial or non-commercial purposes and does not allow rights holders to opt out.

Copyright law has to respond to the realities of the twenty-first century where the growing use of big data and AI tools in research and innovation are necessary to achieve breakthroughs and result from collaboration of different stakeholders – start-ups, SMEs, academia, research groups, governments and business. It should be noted that the main beneficiary of innovative projects is the public. In order for the public to benefit, TDM exceptions should exist for all entities and for all purposes. If the opt out regime is in place, rights holders have control over TDM – they can decide who to grant a licence to or to entirely prohibit the use of their content for TDM. For instance, publishers, who already offer paid-for TDM as value-added services, will be reluctant to grant TDM licences to third parties. Thus, commercial AI developers, journalists, research hubs, and other innovative entities will be at a competitive disadvantage. The opt out regime might cripple innovation for wide range of market players, from large companies to start-ups and individual researchers with a particular emphasis on the game changing field of AI-based innovation. Another downside of the opt out regime is that only a few research organisations will be able to acquire licences for all copyright protected content that is relevant for TDM research. Moreover, comprehensive TDM research projects would be impossible to perform for the majority of research organisations, especially if they have limited access to funding. The opt out mechanism strongly limits the effectiveness of the TDM exception and its ability to promote competitive advantage for companies engaged with AI. The opt out regime would not be able to prevent a situation where dominant market players customarily override exceptions by imposing both contractual and technological measures, thus depriving users of the enjoyment of exceptions and lawful uses. An alternative to an opt out regime would be a fair-remuneration mechanism, implemented by way of an amendment to the CDPA and operated, for instance, by the UK Intellectual Property Office.

4 DABUS Case – A Milestone in Patent Case Law or an Unsuccessful AI Challenge to Patent Law

4.1 AI and Patent Law

Copyright law is not the only area of IP that seems to be relevant with respect of involvement of AI in the creative or inventive process. Patent offices and courts in several countries, including the United Kingdom, have been dealing with the question as to whether artificial intelligence (and thus a non-human) can be an owner of a patent or considered an inventor. Patent offices and courts in several countries have provided – at least tentatively – answers to these questions.

4.2 United Kingdom

In 2018, a team of patent attorneys acting on behalf of an AI scientist, Dr. Stephen Thaler, submitted two patent applications listing an AI system, DABUS, as an inventor. One of the patent applications was for a type of a food container and one for a flashing light. However, Dr. Thaler did not list himself as the inventor. Instead, he listed the DABUS AI system, arguing that DABUS should be granted the patent 'by ownership of the creativity of the machine' – while making clear that DABUS was the inventor, not Mr. Thaler. The UK Intellectual Property Office (UKIPO) told Mr. Thaler that he needed to list a real person as an inventor. Since he did not do so, the UKIPO considered the application as withdrawn and refrained from any further steps. Dr. Thaler claimed that DABUS, which stands for 'Device for Autonomous Bootstrapping of Unified Sentience', invented the flashing light and the food container based on fractal geometry that were listed in the disputed patent applications. The UK was the first country where the patent office's decision was reviewed by a court. On 21 September 2021, Justice Marcus Smith in the High Court of England and Wales dismissed Dr. Thaler's appeal and upheld the UKIPO decision, confirming that AI cannot be listed as an inventor because it is not a person.

The core argument of the High Court was whether a law written for human inventors can be applied to machines. The court ruled against Dr. Thaler. Dr. Thaler even claimed that the artificial inventor DABUS could appreciate its creations, is equipped with learning rules to bind memories, contained with a series of nets, together to produce not only complex concepts, but also the consequences of said concepts, what psychologists would call affective responses. In other words, feelings or sentience was the result.

More recently, the England and Wales Court of Appeals (EWCA) in the case Stephen Thaler and Comptroller General of Patents and Trademarks and Designs from 21 September 2021 by majority (Arnold LJ and Laing LJ; Birss LJ dissenting) upheld the judgment at first instance. Dr. Thaler argued before the EWCA that the definition of the inventor as the 'actual deviser' of an invention pointedly did not refer to the need for the inventor to be a person. While the Patents Act 1977 was clearly written on the assumption that inventors were persons, that was not, an ought not to be, a requirement of the law. The Court of Appeal held that an inventor must be a real human person under the UK law. Lady Justice Elisabeth Laing of the Court of Appeals wrote in her judgment that 'only a person can have rights, a machine cannot'. Patent is a statutory right and can only be granted to a person. Thus, this case was ultimately not about whether an invention is patentable on its own, but rather about whether a machine can have rights. According to the Court of Appeal, it cannot have rights arising out of patent, because it cannot have any other rights. Lord Justice Arnold agreed with the view that according to the Patents Ac 1977, only a person can be an inventor. However, the third Judge, Lord Justice Birss, took a different view in arguing that while machines are not persons, the law did not demand a person to be named as the inventor at all. In his opinion, the fact that in a patent application there is a possibility for not including any inventor, simply means that the Intellectual Property Office does not have to name anyone as an inventor. In his opinion, the UKIPO is not obliged to name anyone or anything as an inventor. While the three judges agreed that AI cannot be listed as an inventor, their opinions differed on whether the UKIPO has sufficient grounds to consider the application as withdrawn. Justice Arnold pointed out that it is not for courts to weigh policy options and to debate what the law ought to be. If Mr. Thaler listed himself as the inventor, such an application would be successful. On the 20th of December 2023, the UK Supreme Court confirmed the view of the Court of Appeals, noting that according to the currenly applicable law, a patent requires disclosure of an inventor, who must be a natural person. Thus, in case of an AI-generated invention without an identifiable human inventor, the invention is unprotectable. The UK Supreme Court noted that if patents are to be granted in respect of inventions made by machines, the 1977 Patents Act will have to be amended.

By the operation of the Patent Cooperation Treaty (PCT), the applications filed in the UKIPO were extended to a number of countries, including the US, Germany, Europe, Australia, South Korea, Japan, Israel, Canada, New Zealand, Taiwan and others. Thus far, patent applications have been rejected not only by the UKIPO, but also by the European Patent Office (EPO), German Patent and Trademark Office, US Patent and Trademark Office (USPTO), and Australian Intellectual Property Office (AUIPO). Dr. Thaler decided to appeal patent registration rejections from the relevant patent offices. Let us have a closer look at applications in other countries.

4.3 USA

In the United States, the DABUS application was had been initially rejected by the United States Patent and Trademark Office (USPTO), which took the view that the definition of the 'inventor' in the Patent Act requires an inventor to be a natural person. Consequently, the USPTO rejected the patent application because no natural person was listed as an inventor. Dr. Thaler appealed the USPTO's decision. On appeal, in September 2021, Judge Leonie Brinkema in the United States District Court for the Eastern District of Virginia upheld the decision of the USPTO that an AI machine cannot be an inventor under the US patent law. In reaching this decision, Brinkema J pointed out that the language used in the Patent Act (35 U.S. Code) and the recent America Invents Act 2011 refers to a human quality, especially in terms such as 'individual', 'himself or herself'. According to Brinkema J, this implies that an inventor must be a human being. The decision was appealed by Dr. Stephen Thaler, but the Supreme Court of the United States declined to hear the appeal in April 2023.

4.4 Germany

In line with the reasoning adopted in the UK and the USA, in Germany, the Examining Section of the German Patent and Trade Mark Office (Deutsches Patent- und Markenamt, hereinafter DPMA), rejected the patent application filed by Dr. Thaler on the grounds that according to Section 6 and Section 37 of the Patent Act an inventor can only be a natural person – a human being with legal capacity under Section 1 of the Civil Code – which does not apply to AI. The crux of the legal problem was whether only a natural person can be named as in inventor within the meaning of Section 37 of the Patent Act. The Federal Patent Court noted in line with courts in other jurisdictions, that only a natural person can be designated as an inventor in a patent application. This conclusion was reached based on a doctrinal understanding of the concept of the 'inventor' and a teleological interpretation of the respective provisions under the German Patent Law. The German Federal Patent

Court viewed the right to be named as an inventor as a personality right, akin to moral rights in copyright. It pointed out that the inventor's right to be named under Sections 37 (1) and 63 of the Patent Act is above all a moral right, and such right can only be borne by humans. The Board stated that the existing provisions reflect 'the decision taken deliberately by the legislature', from which it deduced that 'an AI can never be designated as an inventor or a co-inventor'.

The judgment relied on one of the underlying notions of patent law that an invention is the result of human creativity or ingenuity. However, this seems to contradict the role of Dr. Thaler in the inventive process. Dr. Thaler claimed that DABUS devised the invention at issue completely autonomously and on its own, and that Dr. Thaler had no influence on the task and its solution, which led to the present invention. By the same principle as DABUS was rejected as an inventor, patent offices and courts should have prevented an outcome where Dr. Thaler was designated as the inventor and could be entitled to inventor's rights. The German Federal Patent Court held that the designation of inventorship is an expression of the inventor's personality rights. DABUS can be mentioned in the 'inventor designation', but only as long as Dr. Thaler's name is mentioned, too, and if DABUS has a subsidiary role. There is an irony in the fact that Dr. Thaler became entitled to such rights against his own testimony of not having created an invention himself and performing a rather organisational activity.

The judgment of the Federal Patent Court on the one hand reaffirmed the principle that human creativity underlines the inventor's right to be named and on the other hand, it allowed someone who, in his own words, had no influence on the task and its solution to be named as an inventor, which led to the present invention. If the principle of human creativity was applied consistently and if Dr. Thaler's claim regarding the genesis of the invention had been treated as a statement of fact, rather than an interpretation of the law, the case outcome would be that no one could be designated as the inventor, and, hence, no one could potentially be entitled to the patent for the food container.

4.5 South Africa

The application to register DABUS as an inventor was also made in South Africa. The South African Companies and Intellectual Property Commission became the world's first patent office to award a patent which named AI as the inventor of a product. It should, however, be noted that South Africa has a less rigid patent examination procedure – it does not presently conduct substantive examination of patent applications in the way that the EU, the UK, Australia and the US do.

4.6 Australia

In the light of the aforementioned, the decision of the Federal Court of Australia (FCA) in Thaler v Patent Commissioner seems to be an international outlier. On 30 July 2021, Justice Beach overturned the primary decision of IP Australia and concluded that AI could be listed as an inventor under the Patent's Act. It is the first court decision in the world suggesting that AI can be an inventor under the current patent law. Beach J emphasised that the patent application in question suggests AI as an inventor, not as a patentee. Understandably, since AI does not have a legal personality and cannot be an owner of any rights, it cannot be an owner of a patent. He further emphasised that the understanding of a patentee should clearly be distinguished from an inventor. While only a human or other legal person can be an owner, controller or a patentee, an inventor may be an artificial intelligence system. However, in these circumstances the inventor cannot be the owner, controller or patentee of the patentable invention. An interesting observation was made by Beach J with respect to AI being involved in other areas of intellectual property law. In his opinion, patent law does not require a human 'creator' – this is however, not true with respect to copyright law, because the existence of moral rights in copyright law implies that only a human can be considered an author for the purposes of copyright law. Unlike a patented invention, a copyright-protected work originates by the application of human intellectual effort. Indeed, as discussed in this paper, the concept of authorship would be not be fitting for creations by artificial intelligence, but copyright law has other vehicles to accommodate such creations.

However, this unique and rather controversial decision was reversed in April 2022 by the Federal Court of Australia. The panel of judges pointed out that courts should be cautious about interpreting statutes by reference to what might be considered desirable policy to avoid imputing that policy into legislation and characterising that as the purpose of the legislation. The Court respectfully noted that Dr. Thaler intended to provoke a debate about the extent to which an AI may be an inventor. However, it also suggested that this policy argument "clouded" the question before Beach J.

5 Conclusion

The analysis above shows that despite AI being at the forefront of IP discussions in the past years, legislators, courts, and policy makers are not quite ready yet to accept AI as creators or inventors. The understanding that there is inevitably a 'human behind AI', without whom a subsequent creation or invention by AI would not be possible, seems to prevail. Granting IP rights to AI would raise a host of further legal questions beyond mere IP rights, for instance questions of legal personhood. The question of machines obtaining IP protection should ultimately be decided by policy-makers. Some changes in law and policy can be anticipated, since it is becoming increasingly difficult for humans to discern whether a song or a painting was created or a device was invented by a machine. Ultimately, a policy decision will have to be made as to what type of IP protection should be given to creations and inventions devised by an algorithm with little or no human intervention. In the area of patent, developments may be slow, as it seems that statutory amendments will be needed in order to grant patent rights to AI or recognise AI as an inventor. The latter may be plausible. According to the AIPPI resolution, AI inventions should not be excluded from patent protection per se. At the same time, AI inventions should only be granted patent protection if a natural person is listed as an inventor or co-inventor. However, the input of a natural person can be quite minimal – even limited to the recognition that an output of an AI algorithm constitutes an invention. The UK Government currently holds the position that no change to the UK patent law is being considered because AI is not yet advanced enough to invent without human intervention. However, at the same time, the UK Government noted that the area of patent law will have to be kept under review.

The area of copyright law seems to offer a few options to respond to the challenge of artworks created by AI. This would be particularly by granting AI rights akin to neighbouring (related) rights to copyright, since these rights were created for entities not involved in the creative process, e. g. rights of phonogram producers. Moreover, copyright law has already shown a certain level of flexibility by granting protection to works where there is no human author, i. e. computer-generated works. It seems almost certain that legislators and policy makers will respond to AI challenges to copyright. However, such response will most likely not have a form of a major disruption of IP rights, but rather an incremental change in the form of new rights tailored for AI.

References

AIPPI – Association for the Protection of Intellectual Property, 'Copyright and Artificially Generated Works, Resolution of the 2019 AIPPI World Congress – London, 18 September 2019' <http://114.247.84.87/AIPPI/ztyj/jy/201911/P020191219538152201660.pdf>

——, 'Inventorship of Inventions Made Using Artificial Intelligence, Resolution of the 2020 AIPPI World Congress' <https://aippi.nl/wp-content/uploads/2020/10/Adopted-Resolution-Q272-Patents-Inventorship-of-inventions-made-using-Artificial-Intelligence.pdf>

Aplin T and Davies J, Intellectual Property Law: Text, Cases, and Materials (Fourth Edition, Oxford University Press)

Berne Convention for the Protection of Literary and Artistic Works 29

Čerka P, Grigienė J and Sirbikytė G, 'Liability for Damages Caused by Artificial Intelligence' (2015) 31 Computer Law & Security Review 376

Drexl J and others, 'Artificial Intelligence and Intellectual Property Law – Position Statement of the Max Planck Institute for Innovation and Competition of 9 April 2021 on the Current Debate' (9 April 2021) <https://papers.ssrn.com/abstract=3822924> accessed 15 December 2022

——, 'Technical Aspects of Artificial Intelligence: An Understanding from an Intellectual Property Law Perspective' Max Planck Institute for Innovation and Competition Research Paper Nr. 19 – 13 15

European Parliament, 'Report with Recommendations to the Commission on Civil Law Rules on Robotics' <https://www.europarl.europa.eu/doceo/document/A-8-2017-0005_EN.html> accessed 6 July 2020

'Founder' <https://imagination-engines.com/founder.html> accessed 2 December 2022

Fried I, 'Exclusive: Adobe Will Sell AI-Made Stock Images' (Axios, 5 December 2022) <https://www.axios.com/2022/12/05/adobe-ai-made-stock-images> accessed 6 December 2022

Geiger C, Frosio G and Bulayenko O, 'Text and Data Mining: Articles 3 and 4 of the Directive 2019/790/Eu' [2019] SSRN Electronic Journal <https://www.ssrn.com/abstract=3470653> accessed 28 December 2021

Guadamuz A, 'Do Androids Dream of Electric Copyright? Comparative Analysis of Originality in Artificial Intelligence Generated Works' (2017) 2017 Intellectual Property Quarterly 18

Hartmann C and others, 'Trends and Developments to Artificial Intelligence: Challenges to the Intellectual Property Rights Framework' <https://op.europa.eu/en/publication-detail/-/publication/394345a1-2ecf-11eb-b27b-01aa75ed71a1/language-en>

Harwell D, 'He Used AI to Win a Fine-Arts Competition. Was It Cheating?' (Washington Post, 2 September 2022) <https://www.washingtonpost.com/technology/2022/09/02/midjourney-artificial-intelligence-state-fair-colorado/> accessed 12 December 2022

Hilty RM, Hoffmann J and Scheuerer S, 'Intellectual Property Justification for Artificial Intelligence' 29

Hugenholtz PB, 'The New Copyright Directive: Text and Data Mining (Articles 3 and 4)' (Kluwer Copyright Blog, 24 July 2019) <http://copyrightblog.kluweriplaw.com/2019/07/24/the-new-copyright-directive-text-and-data-mining-articles-3-and-4/> accessed 27 December 2021

Kelly C, 'Australian Artists Accuse Popular AI Imaging App of Stealing Content, Call for Stricter Copyright Laws' The Guardian (11 December 2022) <https://www.theguardian.com/australia-news/2022/dec/12/australian-artists-accuse-popular-ai-imaging-app-of-stealing-content-call-for-stricter-copyright-laws> accessed 12 December 2022

Kim D, 'The Paradox of the DABUS Judgment of the German Federal Patent Court' [2022] GRUR International ikac125

Koempel F, 'UK Music's Legal Expert Outlines Issues With Proposed AI Data Mining' (UK Music, 29 November 2022) <https://www.ukmusic.org/news/uk-musics-legal-expert-outlines-issues-with-proposed-ai-data-mining/> accessed 8 December 2022

Matulionyte R, 'AI as an Inventor: Has the Federal Court of Australia Erred in DABUS?' (2022) 13 JIPITEC <http://www.jipitec.eu/issues/jipitec-13-2-2022/5538>

McCutcheon C, 'Curing the Authorless Void: Protecting Computer-Generated Works Following ICE TV and Phone Directories' (2013) 37 Melbourne University Law Review

McDermott E, 'DABUS Scores Again with Win on AI Inventorship Question in Australia Court' (IPWatchdog.com | Patents & Intellectual Property Law, 2 August 2021) <https://ipwatchdog.com/2021/08/02/dabus-scores-win-ai-inventorship-question-australia-court/id=136304/> accessed 25 November 2022

Metz R, 'These Artists Found out Their Work Was Used to Train AI. Now They're Furious | CNN Business' (CNN, 21 October 2022) <https://www.cnn.com/2022/10/21/tech/artists-ai-images/index.html> accessed 8 December 2022

'Patents and Applications – The Artificial Inventor Project' <https://artificialinventor.com/patent-applications/> accessed 15 December 2022

Ramalho A, 'Will Robots Rule the (Artistic) World? A Proposed Model for the Legal Status of Creations by Artificial Intelligence Systems' (2017) 21 The Journal of Intenet Law 12

———, Intellectual Property Protection for AI-Generated Creations: Europe, United States, Australia, and Japan (Routledge 2021)

Ricketson S, 'The 1992 Horace S. Manges Lecture – People or Machines: The Berne Convention and the Changing Concept of Authorship' 16 Colum-VLA JL & Arts

Senftleben M and Buijtelaar L, 'Robot Creativity: An Incentive-Based Neighboring Rights Approach' [2020] SSRN Electronic Journal <https://www.ssrn.com/abstract=3707741> accessed 17 November 2022

Stassen M, 'Over 1,000 Songs with Human-Mimicking AI Vocals Have Been Released by Tencent Music in China. One of Them Has 100m Streams.' (Music Business Worldwide, 15 November 2022) <https://www.musicbusinessworldwide.com/over-1000-songs-human-mimicking-ai-vocals-have-been-released-by-tencent-music-in-china-one-of-them-has-over-100m-streams/> accessed 12 December 2022

The Government of the United Kingdom, 'Artificial Intelligence and Intellectual Property: Copyright and Patents: Government Response to Consultation' (GOV.UK) <https://www.gov.uk/government/consultations/artificial-intelligence-and-ip-copyright-and-patents/outcome/artificial-intelligence-and-intellectual-property-copyright-and-patents-government-response-to-consultation> accessed 8 December 2022

Trapova and Gervassis Ni, 'UKIPO's Public Consultation on AI and IP – Computer-Generated Works (Part 1)' (Kluwer Copyright Blog, 14 March 2022) <http://copyrightblog.kluweriplaw.com/2022/03/14/ukipos-public-consultation-on-ai-and-ip-computer-generated-works-part-1/> accessed 15 December 2022

UK Intellectual Property Office, 'Artificial Intelligence and Intellectual Property: Copyright and Patents: Government Response to Consultation' (GOV.UK) <https://www.gov.uk/government/consultations/artificial-intelligence-and-ip-copyright-and-patents/outcome/artificial-intelligence-and-intellectual-property-copyright-and-patents-government-response-to-consultation> accessed 13 December 2022

———, 'Government Response to Call for Views on Artificial Intelligence and Intellectual Property' (GOV.UK) <https://www.gov.uk/government/consultations/artificial-intelligence-and-intellectual-property-call-for-views/government-response-to-call-for-views-on-artificial-intelligence-and-intellectual-property> accessed 27 June 2021

van Gompel S, 'Creativity, Autonomy and Personal Touch: A Critical Appraisal of the CJEU's Originality Test for Copyright' in Mireille Eechoud (ed), The Work of Authorship (Amsterdam University Press 2014)

Vanpoucke W, 'Copyright Challenged by Art Created by Artificial Intelligence' (2021) 43 European Intellectual Property Review 12

Vincent J, 'Getty Images Bans AI-Generated Content over Fears of Legal Challenges' (The Verge, 21 September 2022) <https://www.theverge.com/2022/9/21/23364696/getty-images-ai-ban-generated-artwork-illustration-copyright> accessed 2 December 2022

Wiggers K, 'GitHub Launches Copilot for Business Plan as Legal Questions Remain Unresolved' (TechCrunch, 8 December 2022) <https://techcrunch.com/2022/12/08/github-launches-copilot-for-business-plan-as-legal-questions-remain-unresolved/> accessed 12 December 2022

World Intellectual Property Organisation (WIPO), 'The WIPO Conversation on Intellectual Property and Artificial Intelligence' <https://www.wipo.int/

about-ip/en/artificial_intelligence/conversation.html> accessed 11 December 2022

Commissioner of Patents v Thaler (Australia) [2022] Federal Court of Australia FCAFC 62

Decision on patent application GB18169094 and GB18181610, BL O/741/19 [2019] Intellectual Property Office of the United Kingdom BL O/741/19

Dr Stephen L Thaler v Presidentin des Deutschen Patent- und Markenamts, 1 W (pat) 5/21 (Bundespatentgericht (Germany))

Eva Maria Painer v Standard Verlags GmbH [2011] Court of Justice of the European Union ECLI:EU:C:2011:798

Infopaq International A/S v Danske Dagbladens Forening, Case C-5/08, ECLI:EU:C:2009:465 [2009] Court of Justice of the European Union ECLI:EU:C:2009:465

Stephen L Thaler v The Comptroller-General of Patents, Designs and Trade Marks [2020] EWHC 2412 (Pat) [2020]

Thaler v Commissioner of Patents [2021] Federal Court of Australia FCA 879

Thaler v Comptroller General of Patents Trade Marks And Designs [2021] EWCA Civ 1374 (EWCA (Civ))

Thaler v Iancu, et al, No 1:2020cv00903 – Document 33 (ED Va 2021) [2021] United States District Court for the Eastern District of Virginia 1:2020cv00903

Copyright, Designs and Patents Act 1988 (United Kingdom) 1988

Directive 2001/29/EC of the European Parliament and of the Council of 22 May 2001 on the harmonisation of certain aspects of copyright and related rights in the information society, OJ L 167

Directive 2019/790/EU of the European Parliament and of the Council of 17 April 2019 on copyright and related rights in the Digital Single Market and amending Directives 96/9/EC and 2001/29/EC, OJ L 130/92 2019

H.R.1249 – Leahy-Smith America Invents Act

Patent Act 1990 (Act No. 83) (Australia)

Patentgesetz (Germany) – Patent Act as published on 16 December 1980 (Federal Law Gazette 1981 I p. 1), as last amended by Article 4 of the Act of 8 October 2017 (Federal Law Gazette I p. 3546)

Patents Act 1977 (United Kingdom) 1977

Judgment of the Supreme Court, Thaler (Appellant) v Comptroller-General of Patents, Designs and Trade Marks (Respondent) [2023] UKSC 49

An Artificial Intelligence Invention Protection Model

Budi Agus Riswandi and Galih Dwi Ramadhan

1 Introduction

The industrial revolution period reflects the advancement of technology in human civilization. All the industrial revolutions that have occurred have had an impact on economic growth, increased productivity, and high-quality goods and services (Rabeh Morrar, 2017). The industrial revolution is currently in the 4.0 phase which is marked by the proliferation of technology based on computer programs that perform their functions more like a human's ability to think and act, resulting in the technology known as artificial intelligence technology.

The terminology of AI was formally coined by John McCarthy, a computer scientist at a conference in 1956, according to him, it was the

The original version of the chapter has been revised. A correction to this chapter can be found at https://doi.org/10.1007/978-3-031-42576-9_10

B. A. Riswandi (✉) · G. D. Ramadhan
Faculty of Law, Universitas Islam Indonesia, Yogyakarta, Indonesia
e-mail: budiagusr@uii.ac.id

N. Naim (ed.), *Developments in Intellectual Property Strategy*,
https://doi.org/10.1007/978-3-031-42576-9_5

notion of a program, processing and acting on information, such that the result is parallel to how an intelligent person would respond in response to similar input (Tripathi & Ghatak, 2018). In short, the term 'Artificial Intelligence' (hereinafter referred to as AI) refers to those computer systems capable of performing tasks that would normally require some intelligence if done by humans (Intellectual Property Office, 2019).

Along with the industrial revolution era, there was a society era that reflected human social behavior in the use of technological innovations. Society is currently in its 5.0 chapter, which is marked by science and technology by combining virtual and real space in the form of big data, internet of things, and AI in assisting with various human activities. According to the Japanese prime minister, Shinzo Abe said that the concepts of industrial revolution 4.0 and society 5.0 do not have much difference. namely, industrial revolution 4.0 uses AI while society 5.0 focuses on the human component.

AI is a general-purpose technology increasingly present in all aspects of our lives worldwide and across all industry segments. Thus, it cannot be denied that AI is a transformative technology, which has revolutionized many areas of human life. While the technology goes back to the 1950s, the recent exponential increase in data and computing power and improved mathematical models are largely responsible for the current widespread implementation of AI. AI technologies are starting to permeate creative and innovative activities, which until recently were perceived to be solely the remit of humans. The current intellectual property (IP) system was designed to incentivize that human creation and innovation. As AI is operating more autonomously, this raises fundamental questions for the IP system across all IP rights (World Intellectual Property Organization, 2021).

The development of technology in general and AI has led to fundamental changes in the invention process (Simon, 2013). Various examples of currently available and easily recognizable technologies AI technology include Search Engines for websites or e-commerce platforms, Chat Bots, Voice assistants such as Siri for iOS, and Google Assistant, Virtual Travel Assistants, Image Recognition, Humanoid/Robotics such as Tesla Bot, iRobot, and Self-Driving Car. The example above of AI technology can help solve human problems in cyberspace and real space by enabling the combination of software and hardware. Moreover, AI is also being developed to help solve some the world's biggest challenge:

starting from the treatment of chronic diseases or reducing the death rate in traffic accidents, to mitigating climate change or tackling security threats in cyberspace.

However, behind its function in displaying intelligent behavior, AI also has the potential to trigger certain legal problems in certain situations. One of them is related to intellectual property law. Few people pay attention to the challenges that AI presents to intellectual property legal frameworks. Eventhough, the growing importance of AI technology and the gaps in both the copyright and patent systems identified by experts clearly point to the need for further investigation (Burt, 2021).

AI would be defined as the simulation of human intelligence on a machine in order to make the machine efficient to identifying and using the right piece of 'knowledge' at a given step of solving a problem. AI has the ability to think and act like humans, and its complex understanding is a computer program that receives various data as input and then processes it using an algorithm as a method of solving problems using special techniques in the form of minimal machine learning or deep learning to process input data and output results in the form of software that can be operated with an operating system or with hardware whose actions resemble human capabilities.

AI refers to computer programs that can solve problems that previously required human-level programming and coding expertise. AI differs from traditional rule-based programs in that it does not always require a programmer to code all of the rules, instead, it can figure out which rules to use to produce the desired result. This process delegated the heavy lifting to the algorithm, which saved time while also allowing these programs to solve complex problems that would be impractical or impossible to code using the traditional rule-based system (Reinaldo Franqui Machin, 2021). AI can be defined simply as computer program technology. in other words, AI is a form of the recent advancement in computer program technology that exhibits human-like abilities in thinking and acting.

A computer program's main elements are Algorithms, Programming Languages, and Programs, all of which are also owned by AI technology too. The input data is accompanied by special effects or techniques in order for the algorithm to have capabilities such as the way the human brain thinks, and the final output is in the form of software produced by the algorithm, which can provide an action similar to humans in cyberspace and/or realspace with specific/compatible hardware.

In Indonesia, Computer programs are protected by two types of intellectual property laws: namely copyrights and patents. In copyright law, a computer program is referred to as a work provided that the computer program is a set of instructions expressed in the form of language, code, schematics, or in any form intended for the computer to work and can only perform certain functions without special effects or techniques and have no connection with the industrial world. Whereas in patent law, a computer program can be referred to as an invention if the computer program has special effects and techniques in carrying out its function in solving a problem and has a relationship with the industrial world.

Trade-Related Aspects of Intellectual Property Rights (TRIPs) in Article 27 paragraph 1 states that objects that can be patented are any inventions in the form of products or processes in all fields of technology, as long as the invention or technology is still new, contains inventive steps and can be applied in industry.

A patent is an exclusive right granted by the state to an inventor for his invention in the field of technology for a certain period to carry out the invention himself or to give approval to another party to implement it. A patent is the legal right of an inventor to exclude others from making or using a particular invention. This right is sometimes termed an "intellectual property right" and is viewed as an incentive for innovation (Bronwyn H Hall, 2007). An invention is an inventor's idea that is funneled into a specific problem-solving activity in the field of technology, such as the creation of a product or process innovation, or the improvement and development of a product or process. Patent protection is limited the given jurisdiction and is territorial, which means that the patent only protects what is claimed and in the area where the patent is granted which means that patents only provides jurisdictional and regional protection for the desired subject matter in the country or region where the patent is issued (DJKI, 2019).

Patents are state-granted exclusive rights granted to inventors for their technological innovations for a set period of time, after which the creator may use the creation themselves or allow third parties to use it. Furthermore, an innovation is the result of an inventor's idea being applied to a specific technological problem-solving activity, such as the development and enhancement of a product or method.

When AI technology evolves into a sophisticated computer program with a function in solving a problem and a connection to the industrial world, patent law is the appropriate intellectual property law to protect AI inventions. AI inventions are expected to be able to understand unstructured data, reason, learn automatically, and be used to automate the invention process (Blok, 2017).

Aristotelis Tsirigos as WIPO expert in the fields of artificial intelligence, data, intellectual property rights, policy and innovation and Director of the Applied Bioinformatics Laboratories at NYU School of Medicine, in which Aristotelis explained that Artificial Intelligence is a collective computer algorithm that slowly acquires basic human-like abilities in the form of sight, speech, and navigation (World Intellectual Property Organization, 2019).

WIPO gives the characteristics of AI technology, namely having minimal technical effects embedded in the algorithm, the effects of these techniques include; (1) fuzzy logic; (2) probabilistic reasoning; (3) machine learning (classification and regression, support vector machine, neural networks, deep learning, logical and relational learning, probabilistic graphical models, rule learning, instance-based learning, lanent representation, bio-inspired approaches, supervises learning, unsupervised learning, reinforced learning, multi-task learning); (4) ontology engineering; and (5) logic programming (description logistics & expert system).

Based on the above description, AI is classified as an object that can be protected by patent law. However, how does the Indonesian Patent Law System regulate AI as an invention that can be legally protected? Therefore, it would be investigated the protection of AI Inventions in Indonesian Patent Law and compared the protection of AI inventions between Indonesian, United States, and Japanese Patent Laws, as well as identified an Artificial Intelligence Invention Protection Model.

To resolve these issues, normative legal research methods based on the statute approach and comparative approach methods are used. It is hoped that by using normative research methods with a variety of approaches, they will be able to study and comprehend artificial intelligence inventions based on Indonesian patent law and compare them to patent laws in the United States and Japan.

2 Discussion

2.1 Legal Protection of AI Invention Based on Indonesia Patent Law

Essentially, AI is the ability of computer programs to initiate to resemble humans. Basically, and the AI is an innovation in the field of computer programs. Under Law Number 13 of 2016 about Patent (hereafter referred to as the Indonesia Patent Law), There is no specific mention or clearly stated about AI technology or AI inventions as patent objects base on Indonesia Patent law.

In general, the patent object is an invention in the field of technology or what is known as an invention, according to Article 1 Paragraph 1 of Indonesian Patent Law the scope of the type of invention is a product, process, and refinement and development of that product or process. Article 27 Paragraph 1 TRIPS also states that an object that can be patented is any invention, whether it takes the form of products or processes in all fields of technology. and in Article 27 paragraphs 2 and 3 it does not expressly provide exceptions to computer programs or business methods in general from patents and there is no further definition of 'Invention' and 'technology'

In this case, AI is defined as computer programs, and according to the Article 4 paragraph (d) of Indonesia Patent law, if a computer program lacks character, technical effects, and problem solving, it is not an invention and cannot become a patent object. But, if the computer program has a special character, technical effects, and problem solving, it becomes an invention and can become a patent object that is protected by law.

AI is the most recent technology in the field of computer program technology in this era. The distinguishes between ordinary computer programs with AI is that the instruction code used by AI is more complex in writing the code, using algorithms written in a specific programming language, so that the resulting program can solve problems like a human mostly human thinking and acting are predictedable and unpredictable. But an Ordinary computer programs only use codes that have or do not have characters, technical effects, and problem solving and problem solving that are predictable.

AI as an invention of technology can be classified as patented products because AI is a physical entity/object in the form of software that can be used in a variety of existing operating systems or specific operating systems and hardware. AI was invented as part of a computer program invention. A computer program that can be protected by a patent must include programs with characters (an instructions written in a programming language), technical effects, and functions to solve problems, both tangible and intangible, which are inventions that can be patented base on paragraph (d) of Indonesia Patent law. According to IP Module for Patents Issued by Directorat General Intellectual Property of Indonesia in 2019, emphasized that computer program inventions are an example of patent product.

AI as an invention in the field of technology can be classified as patent process for algorithms own by the AI. the process of creating AI through the use of algorithms written in a programming language. The Algorithms written in a programming language have instructions, special technical effects which become source code (input), and then problem solving (output) in the form of human-like thinking and acting abilities. The designed algorithm creates a computer program with human-like abilities, enabling the algorithm be patented as a patent process. Because an algorithm is a process/method for evolving a computer program's capability.

The AI which is a computer program has a problem-solving method in the form of an algorithm owned by a computer program that manages the input data given to produce a certain output and has a technical effect that is embedded into the AI algorithm, for an example that AI technology can solve financial & e-commerce problems. The business methods owned by AI inventions can be divided into offline and online which have an impact on financial business activities (Miyamoto, 2003).

According to Article 4 paragraph (c) number 3 and paragraph (d) of Indonesia Patent Law, AI is an invention that can be granted a patent as an patent product for the software or as the patent process for the algorithm. AI is a computer program that has codes, characters, technical effects, and problem-solving that uses complex/complicated algorithms and is written in a specific programming language. Meanwhile, AI can be patented, but it must meet the substantive requirements known as patentability requirements of patents as well as trace prior art in the form of novelty, inventive step, and industrial applicability.

If AI invention fulfills the patentability requirements for granting patents, which include new inventions, inventive steps, and the ability to be applied in the industry, it is classified as the scope of patent protection with a term protection time of 20 years. Further, if an AI invention is only in the form of development, it is classified as a simple patent protection scope with a 10-year protection period where a simple patent is granted based on an application and each application can only be filed for one invention or one independent claim and cannot be a divisional/fractional application is made, but a simple patent can be converted into a patent if it has several inventions or several independent claims.

Thus, Indonesia's Patent law currently does not clearly state that AI is not a barrier for an inventor to apply for a patent for an invention. Because patent examiners continue to examine using objective and subjective requirements where the requirements are a basis that has been regulated in patent law and make these requirements in examining patents against a cutting-edge invention as is the case with AI inventions to be granted patents or otherwise.

2.2 Comparative Studies on Protection of Artificial Intelligences Invention Between Indonesia, United States, and Japan Patent Law

A comparative study of AI inventions as patent objects in the United States 'Patent Act (35 U.S. Code)' and Japan '(特許法 Tokkyohō)'. The two countries' patent laws explicitly do not mention AI technology, then searches for patent provisions using the term computer program, as previously explained, because AI technology is part of a computer program.

The United States Patent Law only lists computer programs on the part of the patent fee (35 U.S.C.41 and AIA 14) without any explanation regarding computer program inventions and does not mention AI technology as an object of the invention protected under United States patent law. however, in Court Decision No.16/524,350 on April 27, 2020, in the decision of the United States Patent and Trademark Office (USPTO) it has been confirmed that AI technology cannot be an inventor in the United States Patent Law.

In the Japanese Patent Law itself, the Patent Law places provisions for inventions, especially for computer programs, in Art 2 Act No.109 of 2006, the provisions consist of 1 Article with 4 verses.

The United States Patent Law only mentions computer programs, the Japanese Patent Law includes provisions for computer programs and provides an explanation in the contents of the article, and Indonesian patent law also includes provisions for computer programs, although in the Elucidation of Indonesia patent Law. The American Patent Examiner, namely the U.S. The Patent and Trademark Office (USPTO) has issued reference guidelines for examining patents for AI inventions. some definitions of AI in the USPTO guidelines are defined by the U.S. National Institute of Standards and Technology (USPTO, 2020).

The Japanese Patent Examiner, namely the Japan Patent Office, has issued a reference guide for patent examination of AI inventions in the form of a report issued by the Patent Examination Department (Japan Patent Office, 2020). The Indonesian Patent Examiner, namely the Directorate General of Intellectual Property, does not yet have a reference guide for patent examination of AI inventions and is still using the patent examiner module issued in 2019, which in the module does not yet discuss AI inventions.

Although the three countries have not explicitly listed AI inventions in their patent laws, they already have AI inventions that have been protected by patents in their countries, particularly the United States and Japan, which were the first to have protection for AI patent inventions, and Indonesia followed suit in 2019 in terms of granting patents for AI inventions, namely inventions with patent numbers IDS000002530 and IDS000002530.

2.3 An Artificial Intelligence Invention Protection Model

Indeed, AI can help society become modern and even bring about very basic changes, however, its impact on the human condition is clearly uncertain. Therefore, efforts are needed to respond to the various challenges that arise because of the impact of AI intelligently and humanely and take advantage of its positive functions and roles to create a more just and equitable society. Therefore, not a few legal scholars then try to identify a model of AI protection in inventions.

A study conducted by Petr M. Morhat in 2018, claims that AI does not need to be protected through copyright and patent regimes (Rassolov & Chubukova, 2022). To find out the status of legal relationships involving AI, there are at least several types of legal structures and models. First is the machine-centric concept. based on this concept, AI is seen as the legitimate author of the work created. The second is the anthropocentric concept. According to this concept, AI is considered as a tool that humans use in the process of creating intellectual property products. Third is the work-for-hire concept. This concept reveals that AI acts as a "hired worker" creating intellectual property products. Fourth is the hybrid authorship concept, where AI based on this concept is considered as a co-author of human-created intellectual property products. Fifth is the concept of "disappearing" or zero authorship. This concept deals with very difficult situations when the concepts being investigated seem to overlap in different variations.

The Pathetic Dot theory proposed by Lawrence Lessig can be used in providing a form of protection model for AI. Previously, Lawrence Lessig used the Pathetic Dot theory in cyber law regarding cyberspace.

Pathetic Dot theory or other names New Chicago School theory is a theory of socio-economic regulation, this theory discusses how individual lives are governed by four forces: law, norms, market, and technical infrastructure/design (architect). Moreover, in order to form a model of legal protection for AI inventions, it is necessary to consider the legal elements of a multi-level mechanism of responsibility and control over the development of AI itself, where it is considered as a system that is interconnected between technical control, technological control, standardization (sanitary, information, technical, industry standards, etc.), creation of harmonization or unification of technical and technological regulations, as well as organizing a comprehensive "law platform compliance" AI in the form of multilevel "responsibility and control regulators".

Lawrence Lessig identifies four forces that limit an individual's actions, where the four forces represent the sum of what governs individual actions, both directly and indirectly (ex-post & ex-ante). Law, which serves as a sanction and/or provides protection, societal norms, the market, which determines activity based on supply and demand, and architecture, which is a configuration of human behavior/action. Despite their different functions and effects, the four forces work together to regulate or limit the space for individual action/behavior. Norms are constrained by the stigma imposed by the community, markets are constrained by the prices they set, architecture is constrained by the physical burden it imposes, and laws are constrained by the threats posed by the rules.

The four forces of the Pathetic Dot theory can be used to protect an invention, especially the invention of AI as a protection model. The four forces are as follows:

2.3.1 Patent Law as 'Law'

As a form of positive law provided by a country to inventors and their inventions. In this case, for AI protection, patent law is one of the laws that govern technology, particularly inventions. In general, patent law regulates and protects the inventor's exclusive rights to a technological invention. The legislature is working on the patent law provisions. Patent law has guiding principles or principles that are followed and underpin patent law arrangements, particularly in Indonesia with Patent Law Number 13 of 2016.

2.3.2 Social Norm as 'Norms'

Social norms are general habits or rules that guide behavior in a community group and have regional boundaries. The limit of social norms is behavior that is considered appropriate for a community group, which is also known as social rules or social regulations. The values of norms that society owns and believes in can provide an assessment of the usefulness of a technological invention to society.

Technological advancements, particularly inventions, can also influence how society perceives a technological advancement by leveraging social norms that apply in that environment, such as ways, habits, rules of conduct, customs, laws, or fashion. Furthermore, the development of AI with engineering characteristics similar to humans may lead to community disagreements about these inventions.

Thus, social norms control the regulation of AI inventions because the effects and risks of technological developments, particularly AI inventions, can affect social interaction in society because people will use, enjoy, and rely on technology in the future.

2.3.3 Stakeholder as 'Market'

Stakeholders in the form of investors, inventors, distributors, and consumers of a technological invention have an indirect impact on the existence of technology in society, particularly AI. In this case, stakeholders or markets refer to how stakeholders in the business world submit requests (demand) and offers (supply) for a product and/or service, which affect the price to be determined and the form of a product and/or service offered customized on request. Every trade transaction must have demand and supply.

Even though AI inventions are still in the development stage, and the artificial intelligence invention products offered are not widely enjoyed or used by the general public, but rather by people with sufficient financial means, AI are currently in higher supply than market demand. Because the demand is dominated by investors, conglomerates, and governments interested in providing these AI technologies. Market forces, on the other hand, influence inventors' behavior in order for them to present up-to-date inventions.

2.3.4 Source Code of Computer Program as 'Architecture'

A Programmers as individual or group which establish a program/software, the programmers in good faith create and develop technological inventions for human welfare by following a code of ethics for programmers. The architectural aspect referred to in AI inventions is the program code also known as the source code. What is meant by code is a set of computer instructions in the form of an algorithm written in a programming language that functions to give work orders to a computer or a device to perform certain tasks. As previously stated, artificial intelligence inventions are a subset of computer program technology, which also includes algorithms, programming languages, and programs.

Essentially, an AI is a computer program with unique technical components, such that the role of the programmer who provides input instructions (source code) to determine the output of AI becomes the most fundamental force that determines an AI tech's behavior / action.

A programmer has a code of ethics in developing computer technology, one of the codes of ethics issued by the Association for Computing Machinery (ACM), where the code of ethics has been

These four forces together regulate the space for movement-development as well as become a protection for AI inventions. these four powers are applied to be a protection against AI inventions and can also be used to be aware of and avoid the negative effects of AI inventions that can harm humans, especially harm society.

Every year, AI technology is improved so that it has capabilities that are increasingly similar to the ideal abilities of a human (Code Program as architecture). Inventors of AI are granted legal protection for their creations to be morally and economically exploited (Patent Law). The role of the community in assessing the fairness of a technological invention that is constantly evolving each year (Social Norms). Technology investors who collaborate with inventors to develop the most recent technological inventions (Market). Through this AI protection model, adapted from Lawrence Lessig's known as Pathetic Dot theory, it can establish a harmonious relationship between law and technology, especially cutting-edge technology, so that people can enjoy using it in a positive way while the inventor of the technology receives protection for their rights.

3 Conclusion & Suggestion

3.1 Conclusion

Article 27 paragraph 1 of TRIPs states that the object of a patent is an invention in all fields of technology so that cutting-edge inventions such as artificial intelligence inventions are regulated and protected in the national patent law whose provisions are guided by TRIPs. The AI inventions are explicitly not included in the patent laws of Indonesia, the United States, and Japan, but the three patent laws of these countries include provisions regarding computer programs. The patent laws of the three countries in practice have protected AI inventions under the patent laws of their respective countries, although only the United States and Japan have issued patent guidelines for AI inventions.

Lawrence Lessig's Pathetic Dot/New Chicago School theory can be used in creating a protection model for AI invention. The protection model uses 4 powers as protectors, namely the Patent Law "Law" as the protection provided by the State; Social Norms "Norm" as a protection from the cultural aspects of the surrounding community; Market "Market" protection from stakeholders in the business world, and Code Program / Source Code "Architecture" as protection from programmers who develop a computer program technology. these four powers are applied to be a protection against AI and can also be used to be aware of and avoid the negative effects of AI tech

3.2 Suggestion

(a) The renewal of the Indonesian National Patent Law in dealing with the development of AI technology does not need to be carried out in approximately 10 years. Because AI inventions themselves can grant patents based on Law Number 13 of 2016 concerning Patents and based on data on the PDKI-Indonesia website there are 2 inventions based on AI that have been granted patents in 2019 and 2020.

(b) Directorate General Intellectual Property of Indonesia should immediately issue a manual regarding AI artificial intelligence inventions to provide education to patent examiners, academics, and the general public about AI artificial intelligence inventions from the point of view of Indonesian patent law.

References

Blok P. The Inventor's New Tool: Artificial Intelligence-How Does it Fit the European Patent System, European Intellectual Property Review, (2017).

Bronwyn H Hall. Patent and Patent Policy, Oxford Review of Economic Policy, (2007).

DJKI. Modul Kekayaan Intelektual Bidang Paten, Direktorat Jenderal Kekayaan Intelektual Kementerian Hukum & HAM R.I, 2019.

Ilya M. Rassolov and Svetlana G. Chubukova, "Artificial Intelligence and Effective Governance: Legal Framework", Kutafin Law Review Vol. 9 Issues. 2, (2022), p. 314.

Intellectual Property Office, Artificial Intelligence: a worldwide overview of AI Patents and Patenting by the UK AI sector, A Report by the Economics, Research and Evidence team at the Intellectual Property Office United Kingdom, June (2019).

Japan Patent Office. Recent Trends in AI-Related Inventions. Report: Patent Examination Departement, (July 2020).

Jeffrey A. Burt, "The Revolutionary Impact of Artificial Intelligence on the Future of the Legal Profession", Kutafin Law Review, Vol. 8 Issues. 3, (2021), p. 400.

Rabeh Morrar. The Fourth Industrial Revolution (Industry 4.0): A Social Innovation Perspective. Technology Innovation Management Review Vol 7 Issue 11, (November, 2017).

Reinaldo Franqui Machin, "It's Time for the AI Patent: The Case for an Artificial Intelligence Patent Category", Research Gate, October 2021.

Simon B.M. Implications of Technological Advancement for Obviousness, Michigan Telecommunications, and Technology Law Review, (2013).

Swapnil Tripathi & Chandni Ghatak, "Artificial Intelligence and Intellectual Property Law", Christ University Law Journal Vol.7, No.1, (2018).

Tatiana Zaplatina, "the Legal Issues of the Artificial Intelligence, Intellectual Property Rights and Data Protection", Kutafi n University Law Review Vol 6 Issue 1 (2019), p. 45

Tomoko Miyamoto. Patentability of Computer Software and Business Methods. PowerPoint Presentation: delivered at WIPO-MOST Intermediate Training Courses on Practical Intellectual Property Issues in Business, November 10–14, (2003).

USPTO. Inventing AI: Tracing the Diffusion of Artificial Intelligence with U.S. Patents. U.S. Patent and Trademark Office-Office of the Chief Economist IP Data Highlights, 2020.

World Intellectual Property Organization. WIPO Technology Trends 2019: Artificial Intelligence, World Intellectual Property Organization. Geneva-Switzerland: WIPO, 2019.

World Intellectual Property Organization. WIPO Conversation on Intellectual Porpoerty (IP) and Artificial Intelligence, Document Summary by WIPO Secretariat, January, 2021.

Regulation

Indonesia Law No.13 of 2016 concerning Patent

Patent Act 35 U.S. Code

特許法 Tokkyohō

Trade-Related Aspects of Intellectual Property Rights (TRIPs) Agreement.

Care Robots for the Elderly: Legal, Ethical Considerations and Regulatory Strategies

Hui Yun Chan and Anantharaman Muralidharan

1 Introduction

1.1 An Ageing Population

It is projected that by 2030 there will be around 1.4 billion people aged 60 years and older and doubling to 2.1 billion by 2050 (WHO 2022). High income countries such as Japan and the US have a substantial proportion of people who are 60 years and older. As people continue to live longer, people who are 80 years and older will continue to grow to 426 million by 2050 (WHO 2022). Older people live in various types of household settings, ranging from living alone or in communities to those who live in nursing or care homes requiring some form of support in their daily lives. Some of them could be recovering from illness or in

H. Y. Chan (✉) • A. Muralidharan
Centre for Biomedical Ethics, Yong Loo Lin School of Medicine, National University of Singapore, Clinical Research Centre, Singapore, Singapore
e-mail: c.hy@nus.edu.sg; murali@nus.edu.sg

N. Naim (ed.), *Developments in Intellectual Property Strategy*,
https://doi.org/10.1007/978-3-031-42576-9_6

various stages of rehabilitation, while some maintain an active post-retirement life.

An ageing population gives rise to a range of challenges (Van Zaalen et al. 2018). Caring for the elderly requires increasing resources, ranging from caregivers to hospital and community resources, with implications for governments in creating innovative ways to provide continuous care for the ageing population. (Garner et al. 2016; Fulbright 2021; Wilks et al. 2005, 37).

Care robots to the rescue? Prevalence, objections, and concerns regarding care robots

While some of the caregiving labours are outsourced to home-based domestic helpers or live-in nurses and carers, some countries have turned to care robots to assist with care delivery in various capacities to enable the elderly to continue living in their familiar environment and being close to relatives. This development, combined with advancements in artificial intelligence, software engineering and robotics have contributed to progress in developing AI-integrated care robots, pushing the frontiers in care delivery. The 'Elderly Care Giver' concept, for instance, is one of the many longstanding efforts by robotics developers that is geared towards creating multitasking care robots intended as personal assistants for the elderly (van Aerschot and Parviainen 2020). Another type of care robot known as artificial companions are robots with certain levels of intelligence and social skills sufficient to create and sustain long-term relationships with their users (Lim 2012). Their functions range from fulfilling human desires for social connections to providing information and communication, as well as entertainment (Floridi 2008, 652, 653). Other types of robots include those intended for patient rehabilitation and exoskeleton (Tan and Taeihagh 2020). For example, in Singapore various initiatives under the Singapore Health Assistive and Robotics Programme were implemented to integrate care robots with distinct functionalities into different aspects of care provision, ranging from robotic nursing assistant, care assistant and rehabilitation enabling robot to AI-driven robotics for last-last mile delivery (NHIC 2022).

Within Europe and North America, innovations in care robots include those that are designed specifically to fulfil certain tasks. For example, CALONIS, a type of conversational artificial companion is developed for the purpose of engaging and interacting with former soldiers who suffered from brain trauma with cognitive injuries (Wilks et al. 2015). These care robots are programmed to remind the users about appointments, and other activities in their daily lives such as brushing their teeth. CALONIS was modelled after a European Union- funded Senior Companion project which was devised to interact with older people, where these care robots learned about the lives of the elderly via photos, and conversations (Wilks et al. 2015, 258). Other examples include virtual carers for the elderly that aids their daily living and interacts with them (Garner et al. 2016) and LOIS, an elderly companion intended to assist the elderly in managing their needs and monitor their wellbeing on a long-term basis (Fulbright 2021, 403).

Some scholars observed that despite continuous efforts and scientific advancements, the production and use of care robots remain minimal (Hoppe et al. 2022; Fulbright 2021, 404). These could be attributed to manufacturing obstacles that are largely focused on producing robots that carry out simple tasks and research and development of care robots on a smaller scale for specific research purposes that are limited to laboratory settings (Van Aerschot and Parviainen 2020). Gaps in regulation, financing, and data security are among some of the factors influencing low level of trust in using care robots (Hoppe et al. 2022). A change in how care robots is used in the world could potentially aid a wider use of care robots. Van Aerschot and Parviainen (2020, 253) proposed that their use should be framed within the entire care structure encompassing an interdependent system of emotional, social and practical contexts of caregiving. In enabling a widespread use of care robots, they recommended a realistic approach to research that considers market drivers and needs (ibid, 254). This approach could be valuable to inform how regulators shape governance directions for care robots.

What about user experience in interacting with care robots? Some studies reported positive perceptions towards care robots among caregivers in elderly homes (Rantanen et al. 2020; Niemela and Melkas 2019). Adequate training to build competency in interacting with care robots, incentives and usability are said to encourage the adoption of care robots by end users (Frennert et al. 2021). A study exploring users' experience with care robots however revealed the need to be cautious of potential differences between robots that are tested and operated in lab environments and robots that are integrated in home settings (von der Putten et al. 2011, 333, 334). Such findings may affect how users perceive care robots in their home settings, how these interactions change the users and the inclination to build relationships with them in spite of their artificial nature. This seems to support a greater level of comprehensive awareness of underlying beliefs that humans and robots have in creating care robots through an observation of how they interact in the real world, rather than in labs (Heylen et al. 2011). More recent research from Sweden reported stakeholders' doubts about the extent of readiness on the part of their national governance framework within the social and systemic contexts in introducing care robots as part of elder care (Johansson-Pajala and Gustafsson 2022). Further studies exploring perceptions of politicians, insurance organisations and the media in Finland, Sweden and Germany similarly referenced the significance of regulations in supporting the use of care robots in areas such as employment, availability of care robots and financing to developers (Hoppe et al. 2022).

There are, however, some resistance to the use of care robots. Sharkey and Sharkey (2012) raised ethical concerns regarding care robots ranging from reduction in human contact, vulnerabilities arising from loss of control and objectification, loss of privacy, personal liberty, and deception. The inability of care robots to meet the emotional needs of the elderly due to a lack of authentic social interaction and the capability to establish affective relations (Sparrow and Sparrow 2006) are further objections to care robots. It is claimed that robots are incapable of respecting or recognising users and such right to be respected would be undermined should they be allowed (Sparrow 2016, 446). It can be said that a common objection to affective technologies such as social robots and those with close human interactions such as care robots is the existence of associated risks with their use such as vulnerability, interdependency, responsiveness and responsibility, which gives rise to wider implications on caregiving relationships among human beings.

In response to criticisms against care robots, some scholars emphasised the importance of empathy to enable the creation of relationships between care robots and their human users (Leiten et al. 2013; Coeckelbergh 2010). Chan (2021, 638) similarly advocated for care ethics in the design of care robots for its value in fostering trust and its suitability both in the caregiving settings as well as alignment with regulatory guidelines aimed at promoting the safety and security of users, respect for human rights, dignity and privacy and accountability of developers. These recommendations could be seen as attempts at defending against claims that robots are incapable of caring.

These concerns remain as long as robotics continue to develop. Care robots have the potential to affect people's health and safety, as they are placed within the private home environments of the elderly who are likely to be vulnerable. Their daily lives, relationships, object of dependency and experiences could be transformed, thus raising concerns about undesirable effects these robots might have upon the users (McTear et al. 2016, 296, 297). Some research suggested that the aims of robotics should be aligned with human rights principles and relevant ethical values of privacy and autonomy (Vargas et al. 2011, 330). Practical and legal questions such as potential changes to liability regimes where harms occur from the use of care robots are set to become more important as innovations continue (Wilks et al. 2005) as well as questions regarding the legal personality of robots and attribution of responsibilities in the event of harm (Begishev et al. 2021). Whilst their use may be regarded as beneficial from a scientific perspective, important ethical and legal issues need to be considered.

1.2 Ethical Complexities

Vandemeulebrouckea, de Casterleb and Gastmans (2018) in their systematic review of ethical arguments regarding care robots highlighted a range of ethical arguments that are primarily influenced by ethical discussion within aged care settings. The authors proposed the application of 'democratic spaces' that involves all stakeholders in aged care in these debates to better assess their use and reflect on their implications to the users (24). This approach enables a broader consideration of other important influences affecting the relationship between care robots and the elderly, such as issues of reliance, autonomy and responsibility. Two relevant ethical aspects are discussed below.

1.3 Deception and Manipulation

An AI-based robot that is designed to take care of the elderly is intended to perform several tasks. These include administering medicine and treatments, assisting them with daily living tasks and having conversations with them. Fulfilling these tasks requires trust. After all, if the elderly person did not trust the robot they would not cooperate with the robot. For instance, in order for the robot to fulfil its function of administering medicines, the elderly person needs to be able to trust that the mixture of pills he or she is receiving contain the correct medicines at the correct dosages. Distrust here would result in treatment non-compliance and thus the failure of the robot in its task.

It seems natural at this point to find ways to increase the trust that the elderly invests in these robots by various means. Of particular ethical concern, are methods that can be regarded as manipulative or deceptive. In this section, we examine attempts to boost trust in AI by making the robot more humanoid or shaped like cute animals (Siau and Wang 2018) and why such attempts would be considered manipulative. We might initially think that making these AIs look humanoid or similar to cute animals attempts to deceive people into thinking that it is a person or cute animal. However, merely being humanoid or dog-shaped does not mean that one is attempting to deceive people into thinking they are humans or dogs. One would have to go much further in masking its obvious artifice in order to even count as trying to deceive.

While most of us would not find these AIs deceptive, the elderly who may be at some stage of dementia might be deceived. Deception, after all, is ordinarily wrong because it attempts to use someone's capacity to reason for our own ends. This thus fails to respect their capacity to reason. However, for the elderly with dementia, their capacity to reason is impaired. Since respect, in the sense that we are interested in, is a matter of recognition (Darwall 1977), disrespect must be a matter of misrecognition. That is, we disrespect someone only if we treat them as lacking the capacity to reason when they actually possess such capacity. However, here, we are arguably not misrecognising the elderly's capacity to reason, but simply acknowledging that they lack this capacity to an adequate degree and hence should be treated accordingly. Moreover, we are only getting them to trust the robots so that they will willingly take their medicines. Thus, arguably, we are not using them for our own ends, but only getting them to do what they would want to do if their cognitive capacities were intact. While this refinement of the initial argument (viz deception) does not succeed, it and the response to it point to why such ways of increasing trust are objectionable. Firstly, the refinement makes it clear that the "increase trust by deception" assumption is mistaken. If trust was improved via deception, trust would increase only among those who are susceptible to believing that the robots were human like those suffering from dementia. Yet, this is not what was observed in Siau and Wang's study where levels of trust increased for all groups.

Secondly, trust in AI is being generated for reasons that are distinct from the trustworthiness of the AI in question. People are not increasing their trust because they learn something or come to believe something that, if true, would give them more reason to trust AI. Instead, they are being led to trust AI more because it is packaged in certain ways. Looking at this through the lens of nudges can be illuminating. Nudges exploit the ways in which our choices are packaged in order to influence our choices, for good or for ill. To be clear, not all nudges are manipulative in any interesting sense. "Bolding" allergens in an ingredients list, for instance, is a nudge that influences choices by highlighting information that we might be otherwise prone to overlook. Just as not all nudges are manipulative, we might, following Sunstein (2015), note that not every nudge that we might call manipulative is necessarily morally objectionable. For instance, consider an innocuous handphone advertisement which uses catchy music and bright colours to frame the product. While this advertisement is manipulative in that it draws on non-rational considerations to influence choice, it is not objectionably manipulative. Objectionably manipulative nudges are paternalistic, do not provide subjects with salient information, and interfere with deliberation. In this vein, what is wrong with increasing trust in AI by packaging it in humanoid or cute shapes is that it is objectionably manipulative because it seeks to increase trust for no good reason (Sunstein 2015).

Defenders of these types of care robots might object at this point that they are not trying to induce trust by presenting irrelevant considerations.

Instead, they would be attempting to negate irrelevant sources of distrust. After all, even when told that a human and AI are equally reliable at a task, people are inclined to trust the human over the AI (Juravle et al. 2020). The objection here is that this distrust of AI is unjustified and must be engendered by some irrelevant factor. The purpose of shaping AI assistants to more humanoid or cute forms is to remove an inadvertent factor which would influence patients through irrelevant factors. The thought is that instead of illicitly increasing patient trust, they are only preventing the illicit reduction of patient trust. It does not follow from the fact that people trust persons more than AIs that people illicitly decrease their trust in AI. It could be that people illicitly trust people too much or that the gap in trust is justified. In fact, we may have more reason, everything else being equal, to trust people than similarly reliable AIs. After all, while we have reasons of reliability to trust both, we also have moral reasons to trust people, but not AI.

In support of such moral reasons, consider the often heard injunction to give people the benefit of the doubt. For instance, it used to be common, perhaps in kinder times, for members of the opposition to give the winning candidate the benefit of the doubt and also a chance to lead the country (Jones 2004). Such giving of the benefit of the doubt trusting in the face of some evidence of unreliability. This suggests that we think there are some moral reasons to trust persons even when considerations of reliability would suggest not trusting. If there are such moral reasons, we can see why we can permissibly trust persons more than equally reliable AIs. After all, here, the moral reasons stack up. One might object that these moral reasons are reasons of the wrong kind. On this view, trust must be apportioned to reliability. However, this is far from clear. Suppose, for instance, that Alf, a recovering alcoholic, is at an office party and a colleague spills wine on his shirt. When he returns home, his wife, Betty, believes that he has fallen off the wagon despite his protestations otherwise. It seems that Alf can legitimately expect Betty to trust him even when she has evidence (his past alcoholism and the stained shirt) that he is not to be trusted on this matter (Holton 1994). Even if Alf did have a sip of wine, we might think that there is still something problematic about Betty's failure to trust Alf. If Betty has reason to trust Alf, it cannot be based on any sort of evidential or alethic considerations. After all, if they were evidential or alethic, we would think that there is nothing wrong with Betty not trusting Alf. As such, the reasons must be of a moral kind. For instance we might think that Betty owes it to Alf in virtue of him being her husband. Or we might think it is good for Betty to trust Alf so that Alf can learn to develop responsibility or trustworthiness with regards to his drinking problem. These moral reasons make trust apt in these circumstances despite Alf's lack of trustworthiness. This means that moral reasons cannot be the wrong kind of reasons to trust. It follows then that there are at least some cases where we may permissibly trust a person more than an equally reliable AI.

Given that such a trust-gap can be justified, it is not altogether clear that increasing trust by shaping AI assistants in humanoid or cute forms is merely a matter of removing illicit sources of distrust. Instead, it can plausibly, be described as an illicit attempt to engender trust. After all, being humanoid or cute is not any sort of reason at all to trust something however being a person is.

1.4 The 'Zombie Relationship' Problem

One type of use these AI assistants or care robots may be put to is engaging or at least attempting to engage the elderly in conversations. Let us call these types of assistants, conversation bots. In using conversation bots, attention needs to be paid to the value of such assistance. Certainly, one aspect of this value is instrumental: There are a number of health problems and risks associated with social isolation (National Academy of Sciences, Engineering and Medicine 2020). Conversation bots are supposed to be useful in mitigating some of these risks. While the health risks associated with social isolation are serious, mitigating health risks is incidental to the practice of having conversations and social relationships. Instead, the key point of having conversations and social relationships is to connect with a real person on the other side. This aspect matters for two reasons. Firstly, it matters because a large part of the value of having social relationships is grounded in having a relationship with an actual person. Secondly, it matters because people are not likely to engage in conversations purely for health benefits. Instead they engage in conversations in order to communicate with other persons. As we will argue, the health benefits of social contact plausibly arise from the engagement (real or imagined) with other minds. This means that conversational AI may be of dubious value and may even be harmful if used to replace human contact.

Let us first establish the value of there being a person on the other side of the conversation or relationship. To do this, we shall make a small digression: In order to argue against the idea that mental facts were reducible physical facts, David Chalmers (1996) introduces us to the zombie argument. He argues that since we can imagine beings who are physically identical to us, down to the last atom, but who lack conscious experience, mental facts are not reducible to physical facts. Chalmers calls such beings zombies. We are not concerned with whether Chalmers' argument is successful. Instead, we use the concept of zombies for a different purpose.

Imagine that zombies, i.e., beings which look and behave human, but which have no conscious experiences, exist among us. Since they outwardly look and behave human, there is no easy way to distinguish zombies from humans. Consider a situation where one person, Alf, believes himself to be in a relationship with Betty who, unbeknownst to him, is a zombie. Intuitively Alf's relationship with Betty is a sham. In order for the relationship to be real, Alf and Betty need to love each other. However, Betty cannot feel love since she has no conscious experience. Hence, she cannot love Alf. Likewise, Betty's statement that she enjoyed their date is also false since Betty is incapable of enjoyment. After all, while Betty can react and produce appropriate pain and pleasure responses to the respective stimuli, she feels neither pain nor pleasure.

Hence, if Alf were to find out that Betty is a zombie, Alf would have no reason to ask Betty how her day was or ask for her opinion on an issue. He has no reason to keep his promises to her as there is no one to whom he owes the keeping of said promises. He has no reason to be tactful or to compromise on any issue. After all, she has no feelings to be hurt or preferences or values that need accommodation. If this is true in Alf's case, it would be even more so for the elderly who interact with conversation bots. After all, while Alf could choose to continue doing all the usual relationship things because Betty cooks for him, pays half the rent and provides physical intimacy, the elderly have no such pecuniary considerations with respect to a conversation bot. At this point, one might object that conversation bots are no worse than human nurses who are paid to care for (in a practical sense) the elderly but who may not care (in an emotional sense) about their charges (Lancaster 2019). The thought here is that the apparently emotionally rich relationship that an elderly person thinks they have with such a nurse is just as much a sham as it would be if the nurse turned out to be a cleverly disguised robot or a zombie.This objection is mistaken because while the specific emotional relationship the patient believes she has with her nurse is a sham, there still exists a transactional relationship with the nurse. And while such a purely transactional relationship may not be as valuable as one which is more emotionally laden, it is still better than having no kind of relationship at all as would be the case with a care bot. The nurse still has some reason even if only instrumental reason to care about her patient's wellbeing. Moreover, with human nurses, it is possible and perhaps quite common for a more than merely transactional relationship to exist between a nurse and her charge. By contrast, there is no such possibility for a conversation bot or a zombie. In the latter two cases there will necessarily be no transactional relationship let alone an emotionally laden one with the patient. This last point is crucial. Conversation bots do not have minds. Even if we thought that the health benefits would still be some reason to employ such AI assistants, the elderly will not enjoy these benefits if they refuse to engage in conversations with the bots. To see why this might be the case, consider how social isolation can harm people and correspondingly why social interaction staves off those harms. There are two broad classes of causal mediators we might consider: Subjective and objective (National Academy of Sciences, Engineering and Medicine, 2020). A subjective source of harm would be the feeling of loneliness that people experience from knowing that they have no one to talk to, nobody to rely on etc. Insofar as the elderly know that they are talking to robots, it is hard to see how they could not feel lonely since they do not have any relationship with any person. That is to say providing a robot does not seem like it could relieve feelings of loneliness where the patient in question is fully aware that the entity they are conversing with is not a person. Even if it could relieve such feelings, it is not clear that this would be a genuine improvement in patient well-being. After all, feeling lonely is, in fact, the apt response to involuntary solitude. This is similar to how fear is the apt response to something being dangerous and grief is the apt response to the recent loss of a loved one. The mere fact that these are negative emotions does not mean that it is desirable, all things considered, to relieve a person of those feelings without changing the underlying reality which made those feelings apt. If so, even if care-bots could relieve feelings of loneliness among the elderly who are fully aware that it is a robot, this would be perverse.This brings us to the objective causes of harm. Broadly speaking objective causes of harm are those which are caused by the lack of relations with actual persons. It is worth paying attention to the way in which social interaction helps stave off cognitive decline in the elderly. It is well established that having cognitively complex lifestyles can help stave off cognitive decline among the elderly (Festini 2022). Consider now, how we engage in conversations with others. When we talk to others, we try to watch what we say in order to avoid offending the other person. We try to give reasons in order to convince the other person of our own position. We pay attention to the other person's verbal and non-verbal cues in order to understand what the person is trying to say and engage with someone who has their own thoughts and feelings. These tasks can be cognitively demanding. Small wonder, then, that social isolation contributes to cognitive decline. Social isolation deprives people of a significant source of cognitive stimulus and this can hasten cognitive decline.Where the elderly know that these are bots and hence lack minds, they should have no reason to converse with the bots in the way they converse with persons. We perform the cognitively demanding tasks during conversations because our conversational partners are persons and in general we have respect our interlocutors by not needlessly offending them, by giving them reasons for our belief and by trying to understand what they are saying and where they are coming from. In the case where the elderly know that their "interlocutor" is not a person, there is no reason to respect the robot and hence there is no reason to watch what they say, give reasons or pay attention to verbal and non-verbal cues. Without exercising these conversational skills, even if the elderly person does not outright ignore the care-bot, any "conversation" between them is unlikely to contribute to a cognitively complex lifestyle which would aid in staving off cognitive decline. This leaves us with the option of getting the elderly to engage with these AI assistants by deceiving them into thinking that they are conversing with humans. However, as noted, this would be explicitly deceptive and hence impermissible for that reason. If, on the other hand, we remained within ethical boundaries, it is not clear what benefit such conversation bots would have since they are unlikely to be used. Moreover, we can see how replacing nurses with conversation bots may even lead to harm. Whereas a human nurse could genuinely engage the conversational skills of their charges, it is not clear that conversation bots could do the same to the requisite degree outside of a laboratory setting.

The ethical considerations discussed so far examined the relationship complexities between how care robots interact with the elderly that affect how they ought to be designed and developed. An elderly person is not automatically vulnerable and lacking in discerning abilities, however, to prevent deception and manipulation for the elderly who are more likely to be vulnerable (e.g.: those suffering from dementia), care robots could be designed to be less human-like as much as possible to ameliorate the deception and avoid undue attachment to these robots. Further, from a safety perspective, the more human-like the care robot is, the more agile it has to be, which will create hazards when placed in the elderly's home environment. The priority then should be to ensure that these robots are functional, stable, and safe to use rather than aesthetically pleasing.

2 Governance Framework for Care Robots

2.1 Legal Complexities and Considerations

Human robot collaborations intended to improve the quality of life of the elderly with daily interactional functionalities created a slew of legal, ethical, practical and governance concerns. Existing regulatory landscapes remain fuzzy with fragmentary guidance, and ad-hoc standards to address emerging risks. The ideal regulatory regime may yet materialise, and indeed may not be feasible, however the existence of adequate regulatory oversight is crucial given the aim of governance is not to stifle innovations but to ensure that care robots that are marketed and integrated into the lives of elderly are safe for their use and that the elderly users are secure when interacting with care robots. Regulatory bodies continue to face questions such as: how should the legal framework accommodate this new technology? Are existing laws or guidance sufficient to address this new application? These and many related questions will continue to remain important while newer care robots are developed, tested, and marketed to the relevant sectors.

One of the complexities with designing regulatory options is addressing the variety of care robots' functionalities, purposes, software, and hardware compositions. The sophistication and development of care robots meant that it could cross several regulatory scopes, which may give rise to duplicity or in some instances fall outside of the regulatory scope. For example, what types of law should apply to a care robot that assist with the daily routine and can interact with an elderly who is rehabilitating from stroke or managing a progressive illness such as Alzheimer's or dementia? Is the care robot treated as a medical device, or assistive technology capable of providing information useful for medical diagnoses and planning future treatment? When care robots learn more information about the elderly that they cared for and store or transfer such data, it becomes clear that such care robots cannot be precisely classified under laws that govern consumer use of medical devices solely. Further, concerns about security of collected data, privacy of the elderly and families and how these data are managed, maintained and used by healthcare providers require additional consideration of applicable laws regarding data protection and security.

Another relevant consideration is the potential modification to conventional doctor- patient relationships as care robots have seemingly become the intermediary between the elderly patient and healthcare providers, and sometimes an integral part of the treatment or rehabilitation process. Rules relating to doctor-patient confidentiality may have to be extended to these care robots or revised to accommodate the change in this relationship. Other important concerns such as trust, and disclosure of information are similarly affected where care robots enter these healthcare settings (Fosch-Villaronga 2020, 176). It will be seen that Article 9 of GDPR relating to processing of health-related data can become applicable as providers justify the exceptional ground upon which these data processing can occur.

The following sections highlight key concerns that regulators face in designing appropriate governance responses.

2.2 User Health, Safety and Wellbeing

The extent of interactions between care robots and the elderly users affect the latter's physical safety and emotional wellbeing. User health, safety and wellbeing implicate legal considerations (Nambu 2016, 484). The physical appearance of care robots may not mimic an actual human being, however long periods of interactivities may create ethical issues that are hidden at first instance. The issue of deceptiveness of care robots, as discussed above and the inherent vulnerability of elderly who are dependent on these robots as part of their 'normal' functioning in daily routines augment their susceptibility to risks. There is a need to ensure that care robots are safe to use within elderly populations where there is a higher risk and degree of dependency on these robots compared to other sectors. Doubts about the most appropriate classification for care robots – whether they are medical devices or general lifestyle gadgets remain problematic for regulatory purposes as different intended functions attract different liability considerations (Fosch-Villaronga and Mahler 2021). Developers and creators need certainty in comprehending their obligations and protections under applicable standards for safety requirements to enable legal compliance to ensure that users are truly protected (Fosch-Villaronga 2016, 35, 42). Strengthening legislative protections and promoting transparency in how these care robots are used and the effect on the elderly are potential safeguards to ensure the safety and wellbeing of elderly users.

2.3 Data Security and Privacy Protection

Data security, cybersecurity and privacy protection are forefront issues in a big data environment and are particularly crucial in the deployment of care robots (Pierce 2020; Fosch-Villaronga 2020, 173; Fosch-Villaronga and Mahler 2021; Tan and Taeihagh 2020, 15). Care robots that are designed to interact with their users are capable of collecting and storing user information which can be subsequently transferred or communicated to healthcare providers, cloud service providers or manufacturers for further processing and use (Holder et al. 2016, 391). It is this capability that gives rise to data security threat as the collected information may include highly personal and potentially sensitive information such as behavioural, emotional and physiological information, that are liable to be protected from unauthorised disclosure. Data security and privacy risks range from hackers gaining access and creating false profiles to deceive users or their relatives to potential breaches in security protocols and information theft that render users vulnerable to scams (Garner et al. 2016).

It becomes significant that users are made aware of these risks and providers to be responsible in ensuring these risks are addressed or minimised. The elderly should be informed about how their data is collected and used by care robots and caregivers who need to provide treatment or rehabilitation assistance. Nonetheless, the lack of specific guidance about ways to manage security risks despite the existence of cybersecurity certification framework at the European Union level meant that users continue to be at risk as designers and developers are uncertain about the level of minimum standards that they ought to comply with to ensure user safety (Fosch-Villaronga and Mahler 2021). The implications that result from this approach include inadequate IT, software updates and security protocols in places where care robots are used, such as hospitals, care homes and caregivers' settings. New cybersecurity rules for new products such as care robots may be valuable, meanwhile the gap can be addressed by implementing a Manufacturer Disclosure Statement for Medical Device Security (MDS2) form to manage security concerns involving authentication, software upgrades, malware detection (Fosch-Villaronga and Mahler 2021).

Reliance on existing data protection rules such as the GDPR may help determine appropriate roles and responsibilities of data controllers and those who have access to these potentially sensitive information. For example, it is necessary to identify who is the data controller or processor to enable a clear demarcation of obligations in securing and protecting these collected data. Consistent with these obligations, Article 8 on the right to private life is applicable as vast amount of personal data is processed. Prior to collecting data, developers and manufacturers should consider implementing privacy impact assessments, privacy by design, security by design and privacy by default to help address some of the risks arising from processing large amounts of personal data (Holder et al. 2016, 394). The approaches outlined so far support active human interventions in all stages of these processing to properly ensure the lawful collection and processing of these personal data.

2.4 Balancing Innovations, Market and Protecting User Safety

The struggle for policy makers is not new as some studies from Australia and New Zealand have shown that there is limited governmental capacity in steering policy developments to provide oversight for robot technologies arising from limited capabilities in comprehending important repercussions from adopting robotics technologies within a complex system of markets, regulation and technological skills. (Dickinson et al. 2022). Japan grappled with the best way to regulate care robots given that there is an absence of clear definition for care robots within its legal framework (Nambu 2016, 484) as well as technology outpacing regulatory scopes (Iizuka and Ikeda 2021). It is recognised that the difficulty in defining care robots may well stem from concerns that any definitions could potentially create unintended obstacles for innovations and commercialisation strategies (Nambu 2016). The lack of established standards creates difficulties in properly identifying appropriate liability regimes when harms occur from using care robots. In attempts to balance these two interests, Japan introduced its New Growth Strategy in 2010 aimed at ensuring user safety in their interactions with care robots through managing user feedback and contributing to safety standards (ibid, 494, 495). Prior to this Strategy, Japan followed the ISO standards concerning safety guidelines for next generation robots in 2007 (ibid, 488). The publication of Japan's Robot Strategy in 2015 provided further regulatory impetus to support the safe and extensive use robots in everyday life while advancing technological innovations in robotics (ibid, 496). Other suggestions include a greater involvement of various regulatory institutions and creation of new roles for governments in regulating care robots (Iizuka and Ikeda 2021) and more cross departmental collaborations in developing policy response for care robots (Chou et al. 2019). ISO standards appeared to be a favourable option in regulating safety standards for care robots as it has the advantage of enabling various stakeholders to traverse governance processes from an international source point where manufacturers and developers ought to comply with (Iizuka and Ikeda 2021). The situation regarding regulatory difficulties in Japan is not too dissimilar from Taiwan where there is a lack of specific care robot policies and an absence of policy coordination and involvements of various governmental departments (Chou et al. 2019).

The balancing approach is influenced by the purpose envisioned by the regulators when devising regulatory guidance. Reference can be made to the distinctions between the EU certification approach and the US Food and Drug Administration (FDA) policy in regulating medical devices. The EU system (such as a-minimum standards approach in ISO 13482:2014) favours promoting scientific advancements while the FDA is inclined towards protecting consumers from harm, resulting in the differentiated assessment processes (Fosch-Villaronga 2020). One such aspect is in the classifications of care robots, which has remained unsettled. For example, the FDA categorised medical robots as class 2 medical devices (considered as medium risk), such as surgical robotic systems or robots that function to improve the quality of life of patients such as Paro, a robot to help patients with dementia and Alzheimer's. However, the increasing sophistication of intelligence in care robots may add further complexities in the assessment of risks concerning its autonomous nature. This approach is due to augmented developments in robotics, which affect pre-market approval stage costs in testing, resulting in regulators shifting responsibilities to manufacturers in demonstrating safety equivalence with devices already on the market and self-certification (Fosch-Villaronga 2020, 3). Those that fall within a higher risk category will be certified by an external body. This approach however does not resolve the uncertainties in terms of compliance with medical device laws.

Striking an appropriate balance remains complicated as other considerations are influential factors. For example, socio-cultural acceptance to risks from care robots vary across different types of populations, consequently affecting regulatory scope and purpose. In the future, where specific laws are yet to be created, there is an opportunity to include users' and society's preferences about care robots where they are sought to be implemented (Tan and Taeihagh 2020, 15). An approach that prioritises stakeholders' views is more likely to result in an approach that effectively protects users from harm when interacting with new technologies. Research has alluded to the importance of attending to the abilities and needs of users of care robots to ensure designers incorporate safety considerations in designing and implementing these robots (Caleb-Solly et al. 2021). As such, it is crucial to promote evidence gathering and sharing to support stronger regulatory justifications through transparency, advancement of knowledge and cross-agency collaborations combined with effective coordination between national and international regulators in developing regulatory responses (Iizuka and Ikeda 2021). Regulations that did not recognise the mutuality of design, human needs and regulatory aims risk being ineffective, consequently, regulations should be devised in a way that promotes a cyclical nature of communication between developers of new technologies and regulators to improve the regulatory effect towards producing feasible laws (Fosch-Villaronga and Ozcan 2020, 960, 968).

Responsive regulations are important to address some of the complexities in governing these technologies through appropriate governmental stewardship (Dickinson et al. 2022). One of the suggestions as to how care robots can be regulated to balance both interests is for innovations to influence regulation where governments offer responsive governance rather than the traditional top-down approach of regulations affecting innovations (Iizuka and Ikeda 2021, 102335). However, this might be perceived as being closely influenced by market considerations that risk user safety concerns. This approach can be balanced if supported by active stakeholder oversight. Whilst it is important to support innovations, governments have the responsibility to protect the public through regulations that steer innovations towards responsible and publicly appropriate ends. It is preferable that governments play an active regulatory role to govern robotics applications (Palmerini et al. 2016). Dynamic regulatory options that cater to various risks that arise at distinct levels of technological developments may be a viable and feasible option that does not curb innovations yet enable proactive oversight of any issues that arise.

2.5 Regulatory Strategies and Options

The range of regulatory guidance currently available provides further considerations for formulating, revising, or establishing rules that are better tailored to research, development, marketing and use of care robots for the elderly population. Existing guidelines that are applicable to care robots include the IEEE Global Initiative on Ethics of Autonomous and Intelligent Systems, Ethically Aligned Design: A Vision for Prioritizing Human Well-being with Autonomous and Intelligent Systems which focused on general principles of prioritising human rights and human wellbeing in designing and using care robots, developers' accountability and transparency and minimising risks of misuse (IEEE 2019). These principles share some similarities with the British Standards Institute Ethical Design of Robots encompassing risk management, safe design and information for the use of care robots.

The European Commission Robolaw project focused on the legal and ethical concerns regarding consumer health and safety, liability, intellectual property rights and privacy and data protection and protection of basic rights (Fosch-Villaronga 2020, 91, 95), covering the breadth of essential rights ranging from respecting basic tenets of rights, autonomy, privacy, justice and social connectedness. While they are generally applicable to any types of robotics applications, these widely accepted values are relevant to care robots. The Responsible Robotics organisation similarly developed seven principles for responsible robotics that are broadly applicable to care robots: security, safety, privacy, fairness, sustainability, accountability and transparency (FRR 2022). The UN Convention on the Rights of Persons with Disabilities which emphasises respect and support for independent living is applicable for the elderly who have disabilities and may benefit from using care robots. Compliance with established laws and accepted tenets of privacy and related rights remain important in the design process as they affect user safety, especially for vulnerable populations (Chan 2021, 638).

Besides regulatory standards, a more specific-oriented approach in the form of a robot impact assessment for care robots could potentially ameliorate emerging safety risks that arise such as user privacy, data security and liability issues (Fosch-Villaronga 2020, 5). The assessment is underpinned by six principles: impact explanation, comprehensive safety: physical, cognitive safety requirements, consumer robotics: health, consumer protection and environmental protection, liability: current and prospective responsibility, accountability and liability, privacy: privacy and data protection and dignity and broader implications: independence and autonomy, dignity, ethics, and justice (ibid, 97). These principles are consistent with existing international guidance and serve to support their operationalisation. As highlighted earlier, care robots that are used in different settings and contexts create distinct risks and concerns, as such a robot impact assessment is valuable to identify these distinct risks to enable a timelier response. In addition to such functional impact assessment, a regulatory sandbox approach trialled in Singapore is useful to advance innovations but also identify risks that may be hidden when robotics applications are tested in laboratory settings (Tan and Taeihagh 2020). This sandbox approach enables the creation of robotics testbeds and pilots in health clusters across the country, with feedback from users and providers to improve the applications and address concerns that arise.

A broader, overarching type of regulatory approach that strives to embed adaptive elements is an iterative regulatory process proposed by Fosch-Villaronga and Heldeweg (2018). They identified a coordination gap between regulators and robot developers that resulted in disjointed regulatory outcomes that neither effectively support innovations nor protect users of care robots. Pursuant to their iterative regulatory approach, they proposed using forecasts from robot impact assessment for ethico-legal evaluation and actual results of legislative assessment to revise, modify and update the laws. These are intended to create an active evidence-based policy for emerging robotics applications. This means that regulators should understand the attributes that are sought to be regulated i.e., the entire spectrum of stakeholders and subject matter to guide them in developing the laws (ibid, 1269). This could potentially work with other applicable areas of law where care robots are concerned, as they intersect with other aspects of the law such as liability issues, tort, insurance, compensation and medical negligence, hospitals liability and malpractice (Holder et al. 2016, 390). Protecting user safety need not necessarily conflict with scientific innovations. The European Commission Robolaw project initiated in 2012 is primarily innovation-driven but takes a serious view of manufacturers' responsibilities under existing laws covering product liability to ensure that consumers are protected from harm arising from using these products (Holder et al. 2016, 385). Regulators are expected to regard fundamental principles that apply, such as the need for robotics not to compromise human dignity, health, safety and privacy, responsible application of technologies and accountability for liability where robots caused harm (ibid, 386).

The discussion thus far reveals some feasible options for regulating care robots. Ad-hoc type regulations may not sufficiently address the purpose for which care robots are created, (Palmerini et al. 2016) which then affects the adequacy of these laws in addressing the risks from using care robots and their liability to harm caused. In arguing for a product-liability type of regulatory approach for care robots, Palmerini et al. (2016, 80) drew a parallel to the functions of products similar to existing product liability laws, thereby precluding special regulatory regimes. It is correctly observed that liability arising from robotics applications should be regulated in a balanced way that caters to competing interests that are based on real market considerations rather than assumptions (ibid, 83). This approach however does not preclude the creation of new customised rules for certain types of robotics applications, while for other types of applications, existing laws could be applied with appropriate modifications. For example, existing consumer protection legislations may still be relevant where care robots carry risks arising from their design and sale, however further considerations are needed where they test the limits of existing consumer protection laws (Holder et al. 2016, 399). It remains to be seen how this aspect of the law will be applied.

A care robot impact assessment appears to be a feasible option to address emerging or hidden risks presented by care robots, supported by active engagements with all relevant stakeholders to feedback and review the efficacy of laws. The combination of these approaches may mediate some of the legal difficulties in classifying care robots, as it will become clear that the purpose and functionalities of care robots are prioritised in the risk evaluation rather than simply labelling what type of robots they are. Ultimately in ensuring the safe use of care robots, designers, developers, and regulators should have joint proactive roles throughout the lifecycle of care robots, from product design, manufacturing, testing, use and risk monitoring and management. It is through a holistic, multidisciplinary approach to devising regulatory responses in managing the implications from using care robots that enables an adaptive and responsive governance framework to emerging risks and concerns.

3 Conclusion

Care robots are continuing to develop according to the needs, contexts, and use, as well as the level of permissiveness in regulatory landscape where these applications are developed and deployed. As such it is not unusual that their developments are fragmented and highly tailored to the functions they are created to serve. The ethical considerations will continue to remain relevant, as they raised important implications to the stakeholders in its lifecycle, from design, production, testing, implementation and user or market feedback. Research has highlighted the importance of involving end-users in the design and development processes, a valid claim as they are the ones who will be interacting with these care robots on a more frequent basis, and as a result, the effect upon these users could not be underestimated. The elderly population has vulnerabilities which must be addressed in the context in which they use these care robots. Issues such as control of its use, integration in their daily lives, their privacy and security are paramount to ensure their safety in interacting with these care robots. Care robots should meet the purpose for which they are created, thus regulatory frameworks should be designed to offer a measure of assurance to these users that their safety and quality of life are not compromised in favour of scientific advancements. Balancing these two interests is neither straightforward nor simple, as they involve careful deliberation of the technology, the end- users, financing, intellectual property strategies, market needs and developers to guide appropriate standards while allowing flexibility in innovations in a fast-evolving area.

Questions regarding commercialisation and intellectual property protection are increasingly important and any regulatory framework must respond flexibly to these concerns, particularly the ways in which laws are supportive of innovations that benefit the population, while seeking to protect the safety of users. Besides considering the types of regulatory framework, it is equally important to consider the implementation capabilities of countries in regulating care robots, particularly the preparedness of stakeholders in engaging with the implementation. Researchers and markets develop in different paces from the experience of end-users, who are usually perceived as the 'passive' recipient of technological applications and so this risks mismatch of utilities of care robots and why these are introduced into their lives where human carers are available or if they preferred human carers. Bringing elderly end- users to the conversation is a significant first step in ensuring these care robots is designed to function in a way that serves the interests of elderly end-users.

References

Begishev, I., Khisamova Z., & Vasyukov, V. Technological, (2021). Ethical, Environmental and Legal Aspects of Robotics. E3S Web of Conferences, 244, 12028 https://doi.org/10.1051/e3sconf/202124412028EMMFT-2020

Caleb-Solly, P., Harper, C., & Dogramadzi, S. (2021). Standards and Regulations for Physically Assistive Robots. Proceedings of the 2021 IEEE International Conference on Intelligence and Safety for Robotics. Nagoya, Japan, March 4–6, 2021

Chalmers, D. J. (1996). The Conscious Mind: In Search of a Fundamental Theory. Oxford University Press.

Chan, K. Y. G. (2021). Trust in and Ethical Design of Carebots: The Case for Ethics of Care. International Journal of Social Robotics, 13, 629–645, https://doi.org/10.1007/s12369-020-00653-w

Chou, Y-h., Wang, S-y. B., & Lin, Y-t. (2019). Long-term care and technological innovation: the application and policy development of care robots in Taiwan. Journal of Asian Public Policy, 12(1), 104–123, https://doi.org/10.1080/17516234.2018.1492315

Coeckelbergh, M. (2010). Artificial Companions: Empathy and Vulnerability Mirroring in Human-Robot Relations. Studies in Ethics, Law, and Technology, 4(3), Article 2. https://doi.org/10.2202/1941-6008.1126

Darwall, S. L. (1977). Two Kinds of Respect. Ethics, 88(1), 36–49. Retrieved from http://www.jstor.org/stable/2379993

Dickinson, H., Smith, C., Carey, N., & Carey, G. (2022). "We're Still Struggling a Bit to Actually Figure Out What That Means for Government": An Exploration of the Policy Capacity Required to Oversee Robot Technologies in Australia and New Zealand Care Services. Int. J. Environ. Res. Public Health, 19, 4696. https://doi.org/10.3390/ijerph19084696

Festini, S. B. (2022). Busyness, mental engagement, and stress: Relationships to neurocognitive aging and behavior. Frontiers in Aging Neuroscience, 14, 980599. https://doi.org/10.3389/fnagi.2022.980599

Floridi, L. (2008). Artificial Intelligence's New Frontier: Artificial Companions and the Fourth Revolution. Metaphilosophy, 39(4–5), 651–655.

Fosch-Villaronga, E. (2016). ISO 13482:2014 and Its Confusing Categories. Building a Bridge Between Law and Robotics. In Wenger et al. (eds.), New Trends in Medical and Service Robots, Mechanisms and Machine Science (1st ed, pp. 31–44). Springer International Publishing Switzerland. https://doi.org/10.1007/978-3-319-30674-2_3

Fosch-Villaronga, E. (2020). Robots, Healthcare, and the Law Regulating Automation in Personal Care. Routledge.

Fosch-Villaronga, E., & Heldeweg, M. (2018). "Regulation, I presume?" said the robot – Towards an iterative regulatory process for robot governance. Computer Law and Security Review, 34, 1258–1277.

Fosch-Villaronga, E., & Mahler, T. (2021). Cybersecurity, safety and robots: Strengthening the link between cybersecurity and safety in the context of care robots. Computer Law & Security Review, 41, 105528.

Fosch-Villaronga, E., & Özcan, B. (2020). The Progressive Intertwinement Between Design, Human Needs and the Regulation of Care Technology: The Case of Lower-Limb Exoskeletons. International Journal of Social Robotics, 12, 959–972 https://doi.org/10.1007/s12369-019-00537-8

Frennert, S., Aminoff, H., & Östlund, B. (2021). Technological Frames and Care Robots in Eldercare. International Journal of Social Robotics, 13, 311–325, https://doi.org/10.1007/s12369-020-00641-0

Fulbright, R. (2021). A Synthetic Elderly Companion Named Lois. In Q. Gao & J. Zhou (Eds.): HCII, LNCS 12787, (pp. 403–417). Springer Nature Switzerland AG.

Garner, T. A., Powell, W. A., & Carr, V. (2016). Virtual carers for the elderly: A case study review of ethical responsibilities. Digital Health, 2, 1–14, https://doi.org/10.1177/2055207616681173

Heylen, D., op den Akker, R., ter Maat, M., Petta, P., Rank, S., Reidsma, D., & Zwiers, J. (2011) On The Nature Of Engineering Social Artificial Companions. Applied Artificial Intelligence, 25(6), 549–574, https://doi.org/10.1080/08839514.2011.587156

Holton, R. (1994). Deciding to trust, coming to believe. Australasian Journal of Philosophy, 72(1), 63–76. https://doi.org/10.1080/00048409412345881.

Holder, C., Khurana, V., Harrison, F., & Jacobs, L. (2016). Robotics and law: Key legal and regulatory implications of the robotics age (Part I of II). Computer law & Security Review, 32.

Hoppe, J. A., Melkas, H., Pekkarinen, S., Tuisku, O., Hennala, L., Johansson-Pajala, R-M., Gustafsson, C., & Thommes, K. (2022). Perception of Society's Trust in Care Robots by Public Opinion Leaders. International Journal of Human-Computer Interaction, 1–17, https://doi.org/10.1080/10447318.2022.2081283

IEEE. (2019). Ethically Aligned Design: A Vision for Prioritizing Human Well-being with Autonomous and Intelligent Systems. Retrieved Nov 7, 2022, from https://standards.ieee.org/wp-content/uploads/import/documents/other/ead1e.pdf

Iizuka, M., & Ikeda, Y. (2021). Regulation and innovation under the 4th industrial revolution: The case of a healthcare robot, HAL by Cyberdyne. Technovation, 108, 102335.

Johansson-Pajala, R-M., & Gustafsson, C. (2022). Significant challenges when introducing care robots in Swedish elder care. Disability and Rehabilitation: Assistive Technology, 17(2), 166–176, https://doi.org/10.1080/17483107.2020.1773549

Jones, J. (2004, February 20). Public Gives Bush Benefit of Doubt on National Guard Service. Princeton, New Jersey. Retrieved from https://news.gallup.com/poll/10690/public-gives-bush-benefit-doubt-national-guard-service.aspx

Juravle, G., Boudouraki, A., Terziyska, M., & Rezlescu, C. (2020). Trust in Artificial Intelligence for Medical Diagnosis. Progress in Brain Research, 253, 263–282. https://doi.org/10.1016/bs.pbr.2020.06.006

Lancaster, K. (2019). The robotic touch: Why there is no good reason to prefer human nurses to carebots. Philosophy in the Contemporary World, 25(2), 88–109.

Leiten, I., Pereira, A., Mascarenhas, S., Martinho, C., Prada, R., & Paiva, A. (2013). The influence of empathy in human–robot relations. Int. J. Human-Computer Studies, 71, 250–260.

Lim, M.Y. (2012). Memory models for intelligent social companions. In Zacarias, M., de Oliveira, J.V. (eds.) Human-Computer Interaction. SCI, 396, (pp. 241–262). Springer, Heidelberg.

McTear, M. et al., (2016). Conversational Interfaces: Devices, Wearables, Virtual Agents, and Robots, (pp. 283–308). Springer International Publishing Switzerland https://doi.org/10.1007/978-3-319-32967-3_13

Nambu, T. (2016). Legal regulations and public policies for next-generation robots in Japan. AI & Soc, 31, 483–500.

National Academy of Sciences, Engineering and Medicine. (2020). Social Isolation and Loneliness in Older Adults: Opportunities for the Healthcare System. Washington, DC: The National Academies Press. https://doi.org/10.17226/25663

National Health Innovation Centre. (2022). Singapore Health Assistive and Robotics Programme Grant. Retrieved Nov 2, 2022, from https://nhic.sg/web/index.php/collaborations/sharp-projects

Niemelä, M., & Melkas, H. (2019). Robots as Social and Physical Assistants in Elderly Care. In M. Toivonen, & E. Saari (eds.), Human-Centered Digitalization and Services, Translational Systems Sciences (1st ed., pp. 177–197). Springer Nature Singapore Pte Ltd. https://doi.org/10.1007/978-981-13-7725-9_10

Palmerini, E., Bertolini, A., Battaglia, F., Koops, B.-J., Carnevale, A., & Salvini, P. (2016). RoboLaw: Towards a European framework for robotics regulation. Robotics and Autonomous Systems, 86, 78–85, https://doi.org/10.1016/j.robot.2016.08.0260921-8890

Pierce, R. (2020). Robots, the Alzheimer patient, and the GDPR: Policy and privacy considerations for the use of robots in care, treatment, and diagnosis. Alzheimer's Dement, 16(Suppl. 10), e043261.

Rantanen, T., Leppälahti, T., Porokuokka, J., & Heikkinen, S. (2020). Impacts of a Care Robotics Project on Finnish Home Care Workers' Attitudes towards Robots. Int. J. Environ. Res. Public Health, 17, 7176; https://doi.org/10.3390/ijerph17197176

Responsible Robotics. (2022). Assessment principles. Retrieved Nov 2, 2022, from https://responsiblerobotics.org/quality-mark/assessment-principles/

Sharkey, A., & Sharkey, N. (2012). Granny and the robots: ethical issues in robot care for the elderly. Ethics Inf Technol, 14, 27–40.

Siau, K., & Wang, W. (2018). Building Trust in Artificial Intelligence and Robotics. Cutter Business Technology Journal, 31(2), 47–53.
Sparrow, R. (2016). Robots in aged care: a dystopian future? AI & Soc, 31, 445–454.
Sparrow, R., & Sparrow, L. (2006). In the hands of machines? The future of aged care. Mind Mach, 16, 141–161, https://doi.org/10.1007/s11023-006-9030-6
Sunstein, C. R. (2015). The Ethics of Nudging. Yale Journal on Regulation, 32, 413–450.
Tan, S. Y., & Taeihagh, A. (2020). Governing the adoption of robotics and autonomous systems in long-term care in Singapore. Policy And Society, 1–20 https://doi.org/10.1080/14494035.2020.1782627
Van Zaalen, Y., McDonnell, M., Mikołajczyk, B., Buttigieg, S., del Carmen Requena, M., & Holtkamp, F. (2018). Technology implementation in delivery of healthcare to older people: how can the least voiced in society be heard? Journal of Enabling Technologies, 12(2), 76–90.
Van Aerschot, L., & Parviainen, J. (2020). Robots responding to care needs? A multitasking care robot pursued for 25 years, available products offer simple entertainment and instrumental assistance. Ethics and Information Technology, 22, 247–256 https://doi.org/10.1007/s10676-020-09536-0
Vandemeulebrouckea, T., de Casterléb, B. D., & Gastmans, C. (2018). The use of care robots in aged care: A systematic review of argument-based ethics literature. Archives of Gerontology and Geriatrics, 74, 15–25.
Vargas, P. A., Fernaeus, Y., Lim, M. Y., Enz, S., Ho, W. C., Jacobsson, M., & Ayllet, R. (2011). Advocating an ethical memory model for artificial companions from a human-centred perspective. AI & Soc, 26, 329–337.
Von der Pütten, A. M., Krämer, N. C., & Eimler, S. C. (2011). Living with a Robot Companion – Empirical Study on the Interaction with an Artificial Health Advisor. ICMI'11, November 14–18, ACM, 327–334, 978-1-4503-0641-6/11/11
WHO. (2022, October 1). Ageing and health. Retrieved Nov 7, 2022, from https://www.who.int/news-room/fact-sheets/detail/ageing-and-health
Wilks, Y., Bengio, S., & Bourlard, H. (Eds.) (2005). Artificial Companions MLMI 2004, LNCS 3361, pp. 36–45, Springer-Verlag Berlin Heidelberg.
Wilks, Y., Jasiewicz, J. M., Catizone, R., Galescu, L., Martinez, K. M., & Rugs, D. (2015). CALONIS: An Artificial Companion Within a Smart Home for the Care of Cognitively Impaired Patients. In C. Bodine et al. (Eds.): ICOST 2014, LNCS 8456, (pp. 255–260). Springer International Publishing Switzerland. https://doi.org/10.1007/978-3-319-14424-5_30

An Examination of the Tangible Value of IP Financing for Companies and Businesses

Nadia Naim

Intellectual or intangible assets are today recognised by many companies as their most important resource. Without intellectual property rights [IPR] many innovative ventures have nothing to sell or licence. In contemporary knowledge-intensive economies, from the world's largest and most powerful companies to the smallest small to medium sized enterprises, the exploitation of intellectual assets; copyright, patents, trademarks, designs and know-how are essential to business and the creative industries. However intellectual property is rarely sufficient, of itself, to create businesses or, indeed, to create significant economic value, it needs to be incorporated into a commercialisation plan. A successful future for IP financing is a significant step in further development of the IP-based economy. An IP audit is a systematic review of all IP assets (registered and unregistered) created, owned, used and/or licensed by a business. IP audits are important to identify how good the processes to capture and manage IP are. Questions around controlling leakages to customers and

N. Naim (✉)
Law and Social Sciences, Aston University, Birmingham, UK
e-mail: n.naim@aston.ac.uk

N. Naim (ed.), *Developments in Intellectual Property Strategy*,
https://doi.org/10.1007/978-3-031-42576-9_7

industry, filling in the gaps in the IP portfolio to support future products and assets and most importantly, are we protecting the right IP assets in the right way are all questions to be explored in this chapter.

1 IP and Business

IP occurs through a business and every business owns IP in varying forms and to various values. Whether starting-up, spinning-out or developing an existing business, research and development will create volumes of potentially valuable IP. This could be looking at a brand-new product from the outset to incremental improvements along the way. Identifying what has been done at each stage and assessing what IP might exist will allow a business to decide on whether or not to tie down the IP. Existing WIPO Treaties, including the Berne Convention, provide the framework for creators to monetise their creations, however the necessary regulatory frameworks and mechanism for IP financing unlocking quantifiable value to grow businesses, have been nascent (WIPO 2021).

Regardless of being a high or low tech business, a brand could become the most valuable asset a business owns as it is often highly influential to customers. Whether this is the name of the business itself, or a range of products being marketed and sold. marketing a business many aspects of IP will be created, whether this is through TV adverts, social media clips, blogs or banners or leaflets at exhibitions. Understanding who creates and owns the rights to what can be important to ensuring the valuable assets within the business are maintained, to protecting against accidental infringement on others' rights, the management of IP rights is a vital lever to business growth and success (Tang 2022).

IP protects competitive advantage as it creates barriers to entry and provides freedom to operate, it can support customer lock-in, and as a result, aligns security with purpose of funds and drivers of cash flows. It enables scale up for IP rich businesses as unlike tangible assets, intangibles like IP do not wear out with use. In fact, the more widely IP is adopted, the more valuable it becomes and therefore, when better understood, could be the main focus for company investment. There is already considerable scale-up expenditure invested in IP rights through research and development, software, data, process improvement and training. Management and investors are well motivated to maintain and retain it, even if difficulties arise with competitors or in more severe cases, litigation proceedings (Brassell 2022). Thus, the IP audit and valuation mechanisms can enhance a business portfolio by creating an IP business strategy for maintaining and exploiting its IP rights.

1.1 What Is an IP Audit?

Intellectual property fuels the creative economy, knowledge-based assets underpin the revenue generated by IP rich companies and could be a vital competitive edge for start-ups and businesses (Durant 2021). The IP audit is a systematic review of all the IP assets a company owns, both registered and unregistered as well as any licencing agreements, to quantify the value that the IP rights add to the overall business finances and strategy. An IP audit that is too broad or doesn't align to the business vision will not be of value. Many companies are able to utilise their IP value as part of their exit strategy, for example, Cadbury's sold their business for $11.5 billion in 2010. Forty-one percent of Cadbury's enterprise value was attributed to its trademark portfolio when the US company Kraft successfully took over the historic British chocolatiers company. The extent to which Cadbury secured all of it various IP assets, especially its trademarks, highlights the value IP can add to the balance sheet and more importantly, how it is monetised to add significant value to the company (Millien 2014).

Away from the multimillion pound companies, with the necessary revenue to not only invest in creating their IP rights, but also protecting them, the focus of this chapter will be on how to better understand the purpose of an audit for the benefit of the whole business sector. For most start ups and new businesses, the prospect of protecting your IP can be exceptionally daunting. What exactly is involved, when is an IP audit needed, how is it performed and how does an audit inform the overall business policy and strategy (Singh 2021). Let's start with the why, IP gives businesses a much needed competitive advantage, not only against economic free riders, but also as a litigation tool to recover losses and other civil law remedies.

1.2 Processes to Identify, Capture and Manage IP

An audit allows a company to know what its core assets are, control mechanisms, actions to strengthen and monetise the company's IP and review non-disclosure agreements, confidentiality contracts and IP licensing arrangements. External investment and financing can be challenging for businesses wishing to expand or avoid an insolvency issue given the hesitancy in the financial sector to approve financial loans against intangible assets. Land & property are tangible commodities that can be more easily quantified by lenders and valued against established banking lending practices. Since the financial crash of 2007, banks and financial institutions are under stringent monitoring and are generally averse to non-conventional risk in asset-based financial lending. However, where a company can demonstrate it has protected its intangible assets and the competitive advantage gained through patents, copyright, and confidentiality agreements, are adequately protected and accounted for in an IP audit and it can be demonstrated that they underpin revenues and forecasts, then banks or investors will consider taking security over them. The diligence-backed IP audit can demonstrate how a company's IP portfolio clearly underpins its products & services and drives the financial growth of the business. Further, where the IP audit incorporates risk assessments for the level of protection for current and upcoming products and services, the higher the likelihood of success with investors and financial institutions. When possible recovery value can be identified from licensing and sale of assets, and subsequently implemented, lenders are more reassured that risks have been mitigated as part of the exit strategy.

Investment in IP development for growing a business can be costly especially where there are different divisions or business streams. As attractive as successful innovation and entrepreneurship is to all businesses, there is a significant investment needed in the form of research and development which more often than not, can have a costly number of failures before successful IP rights are created. Businesses rely on

Intellectual Property valuations to make informed decisions about Intellectual Property protection, return on investment on marketing, research and development, mergers, acquisitions and licensing to establish to lenders that the company has protected the relevant intellectual property assets that are core assets for the securement of future cash flows (UK IPO 2014).

1.3 Contents of an IP Audit

An audit allows for a review of all confidentiality policies to make sure that they are relevant and appropriate. Identify what IP relates to each product and whether the assigned IP right will last the lifetime of the product and capture new products that are in the development stage. Along with this, the contents must cover the likelihood of infringement and robust monitoring mechanisms for the llikelihood of discovering infringement. The audit will establish whether the appropriate IP policies and procedures are in place for the IP rights identified, their validity and status. Identifying the most valuable rights with who is responsible for the corresponding IP policies are needed to further the IP strategy in line with the business plan and to decide what assets should be protected. Procedures are needed to ensure that all IP rights are logged, maintained, and protected. This could be through licensing agreements and legally binding terms that are to be adhered to.

Starting with registered IP assets, primarily, patents, designs and trademarks, a checklist is created to identify a full list of all registered and pending assets, countries in which they are or will be registered, a record of all maintenance fees and dates of renewal. For patents and design rights, a record of inventors and designers with filing dates and numbers, status and expiry date. The IP audit checklist should identify product lines and brands to which each is relevant. (Bainbridge and Howell 2014). A fit for purpose IP audit covers, the management of IP assets, commercialisation, ownership of IP rights, how best to harvest IP, licensing and franchising agreements, insurance, valuation, tax relief advice and fees for IP services in the UK and abroad.

1.4 Patents Audit

The first step is to identify what patents the business has by listing all registered and pending assets. This includes countries in which they are registered or will be registered. Patent registration is the most expensive of all the IP assets and as such requires a patent attorney. For the IP audit, patents that are filed and/or approved need a record of all fees and details of the inventors or designers. Filing dates and numbers with status and expiry date can be aligned to identifiable product lines to which each invention or design is relevant to. Patents are international in nature, and are covered by TRIPS (Articles 27 and 28). In the UK, A full patent application under Patent Act 1977 must contain a request for the grant of a patent and an abstract which gives technical information, in the form of a specification about the invention and the field to which it contributes. The function of the invention needs to be clear and precise to grant a monopoly right (Strix Ltd v Otter Controls Ltd [1995]). A priority date is then given as the date on which an application is filed and the duration of the patent is calculated from that date. The UK patent will only apply in the UK and an analysis of the territorial reach of the patent is needed as part of the audit determine whether international protection is necessary and of value.

The patent process involves a series of steps; starting with the application form and the request for a search from the UK IPO, the Preliminary examination is regulated by section 15A, PA 1977 with an 18 month turnaround window, publication is 18 months from the priority date, followed by Substantive examination, a period for amendments and if successful, the IPO grants the patent. The purpose of the audit is to consult relevant patent databases and create a list of any competing patents that are used by third parties.

1.5 Design Rights Audit

Design rights in the UK can be registered or unregistered. Design rights that can be registered, share some features with patent law, in a very broad sense, and applies to designs that have or are intended to have eye-appeal.

These designs can be described as aesthetic. The other system of design protection is called the design right and is provided for along copyright lines. This right applies to designs that can be said to be functional in nature such as a new design for an engine cover or a plastic printer ink cartridge. It can, however, also apply to many registrable designs and there is a large overlap between the two forms of design rights. Both forms of design right relate to the design aspects of the shape or configuration of an article and, for registered designs only, also to pattern and ornament.

A design is the outward appearance of the whole or parts of a product. A product can be any industrial or handicraft item. Examples of design features include lines, colours and shapes. Designs must be novel or new and no other identical design has been made available to the public. The design needs to have individual character. Important for the audit checklist is to establish whether the same 'overall impression' on the 'informed user' has already been disclosed. Some designs are excluded from protection by law because they run counter to public order and morality, and exclusions need to be checked. When a product must be a certain shape to perform a function, then it does not have design freedom, i.e. the part of a key that fits into the lock that it was designed with.

The unregistered form of the design right works similarly to copyright and is discussed below. Keeping a record of owning the right, who has designed it and when, is evidential proof for owning the right, whereas with a registered right you have a certificate to provide evidence that the right exists. Design rights have significantly shorter terms and criteria for protection, dependent upon time from marketing and creation (UK IPO).

1.6 Trademarks Audit

Article 3 of EU Trade Marks Directive removed the requirement of graphical representation (Regulation (EU) 2015/2424). Integral to the trademarks audit is to ensure a registered trade mark or upcoming trade mark consist of a sign, in particular words, including personal names, or designs, letters, numerals, colours, the shape of goods or of the packaging of goods, or sounds, provided that such signs are capable of: (a) distinguishing the goods or services of one undertaking from those of other undertakings; and (b)being represented on the register in a manner which enables the competent authorities and the public to determine the clear and precise subject matter of the protection afforded to its proprietor. The representation needs to be "clear, precise, self-contained, easily accessible, intelligible, durable and objective" (Section 13 in the preamble of the Directive).

The application process can be handled internally or with a trademark attorney. A request for registration can be made to the relevant IP office, with information about the identity and address of the applicant, statement of goods/services which are the subject of the trademark registration, representation of the mark and the statement will be used. The applicant receives a filing date, the registrar examines the application against absolute and relative grounds for refusal (Trade Mark Act 1994, UK).

Section 3 of the Trade Mark 1994 Act gives the absolute grounds for refusal (derived directly from Article 3 of EU Directive 89/104/EEC), and sets out categories of signs which cannot be registered. However, signs in 3 of these categories are capable of registration if accompanied by proof of secondary (or acquired) meaning.

The 3 categories of marks which cannot be registered unless they show proof of a secondary or acquired meaning to give a distinctive character as a result of use are:-

S.3(1)b – Trademarks which are devoid of any distinctive character.

S.3(1)c – Trademarks which consist exclusively of signs or indications which are descriptive of the goods or services themselves.

S.3(1)d – Trademarks which consist exclusively of signs or indications which have become generic terms in general language or the specific market sector. (Trade Mark Act 1994. UK).

When a trade mark application is examined at the Intellectual Property Office, it may attract objections based on one or more of these categories. The types of marks that can fall into the above categories are words/signs/devices/shapes which are wholly descriptive of the product.

The registrar will also examine existing marks, and trade marks may also be refused registration on the basis of relative grounds. This is concerned with the effect of registration that the proposed mark may have on other pre-existing marks. It used to be the case that the UK Trade Mark registry raised these grounds at the application stage. However, it is now left to owners of trade mark registrations to oppose applications through publication in the trademark journal. The trade mark application is then open to public inspection and possible objection for a period of three months from the date of publication.

If, as occasionally happens, an objection is raised by a third party against the application, then the matter has to be considered and appropriate action taken. It may be possible to deal with such an objection in a relatively simple exchange of correspondence. On other occasions, the ensuing opposition proceedings can be long and complicated.

If there is no objection, or any objection has been resolved, then the application can proceed to registration on completion of certain formalities at the Trade Mark Registry. A registration certificate is then issued and the trade mark is placed on the Register for a period of ten years from the date of application. After that, it can be renewed indefinitely.

For classifications of the trade mark, the Nice classification system can be utilised to ascertain the classes of goods for which this mark should be applied and nationally, IP offices have a trade mark search to allow for comparison with existing classified marks. (Trade Mark Search, UK IPO).

2 Passing Off

As well as trade mark protection, the audit benefits from an understanding of brand power and how to protect unregistered marks. Brand power accumulates significant goodwill which can enable businesses to successfully extend the brand to new products, gain trade leverage in the competition for retailers' distribution points and take advantage of potential cost savings in the promotion of new products in comparison to potential new entrants or competitors with less brand power. In addition to the brand's reputation amongst consumers,

Despite the availability of statutory protection for brands under the Trade Marks Act, the common law tort of passing off remains important, for at least two reasons. First, many small businesses are not equipped or aware that they should register their trade marks early, and as a result, may be forced to rely on passing off. Secondly, a mark which is otherwise invalid or unregistrable, as discussed above on absolute and relative grounds for refusal, may be able to gain some level of protection through passing off.

Passing off has recently proved useful in combatting 'cybersquatting', the practice of registering Internet domain names containing company names or trade mark names by persons hoping to sell the names at grossly inflated prices to the relevant companies or trade mark proprietors. As a common law tort, it aligns to the concept of unfair competition. It is recognised in international law under the Paris Convention for the protection of Industrial Property.

3 Measuring the Value of Goodwill

In IRC v Muller & Co's Margarine Ltd [1901], goodwill was defined as the attractive force which brings in custom, or "whatever adds value to a business". Goodwill can be seen as value added elements which lead consumers to purchase a trader's goods/services. It is not the same as reputation, as reputation can occur without a consumer purchase. Consequently, goodwill can be seen to exist in company/product names, devices/logos, and the particular way in which a product is packaged. Goodwill needs to be established by evidence. One of the main issues in establishing goodwill is its locality and scope. For example, a restaurant with an excellent reputation for food is fixed in one location, any goodwill it achieves is unlikely to be nationwide. However, companies have been able to show goodwill even if they do not trade in a particular locality, region or even country (Sheraton Corp. of America v Sheraton Motels [1964]).

To quantify the goodwill, a business can satisfy goodwill by demonstrating a reputation and a customer base (Countess Housewares v Addis) and it can also exist in things such as a business name, devices and its get-up. The case of Coca-Cola v Barr found in favour of Coca-Cola and held the style of Coca-Cola's bottle was part of their get-up and subsequently demonstrated their goodwill. Together with goodwill, the tests for passing off require a misrepresentation and consequential damage to occur.

3.1 Hidden Assets

Hidden assets can include know-how, trade secrets, databases, mailing lists, customer lists, contractual agreements, creation of websites, domains and training programmes. For trade secrets and confidential information, one named person should be in control of all relevant information, and it should be recorded who this person is. They should be tasked with identifying, grading, tagging, and giving sensitive information an appropriate level of protection. Confidential information should be classified according to its importance to the business and each grade should have polices dealing with access and sharing of that type of information, and it must be stored appropriately to retain its status. Employees must know what is regarded as a trade secret and confidentiality agreements can be included in contracts of employment. Accurate and detailed contractual clauses can stipulate the importance of adhering to the confidentiality policies and understanding the consequences of breaching the terms of the contract. The law of breach of confidence developed in equity as a way of protecting confidential information by preventing its use by employees to whom the information has been divulged in confidence or avoid further unapproved disclosure. Highly confidential information should be restricted on a need-to-know basis, it would need to be stored safely and password protected, with secure records kept.

3.2 Copyright Audit

Given that copyright is an unregistered IP asset, for auditing purposes, a copyright policy will be the central document to accurately record and protect all copyright works. Separate works can be categorised dependent upon the core copyright works for the business and could include software, web pages, training materials and advertisements. Meticulous record keeping is required for unregistered assets and the copyright policy can include time sensitive information. For example, the date the work was created and where, determines the length of protection and provides evidence if there is a dispute or suspected infringement. Linking back to the employment contract, any copyright created by employees would need to have a valid clause in place as to who owns the work. This would determine who is named as the author with information as to their status. If commissioned, the authorship would most commonly be retained by the company and any assignments or licences of the copyright to be agreed with the necessary terms (Copyright, Design and Patents Act 1988).

4 IP Due Diligence

Once the IP audit is complete and there is a clear record of all IP assets, IP due diligence can provide a snapshot of where the IP assets and liabilities, in relation to an IP transaction, are identified and verified. It is narrower in scope than an audit as it relates only to the IP rights that are relevant to the transaction. It is tailored to an event, such as purchasing of a company or investment purposes. Further, it can involve buying or selling IP, litigation, filing patents, the development or launch of a new product or as an exit strategy.

Key considerations are drawn from the IP audit and an assessment of the authority to use, the validity, duration, strengths and weaknesses of the rights, the vulnerability to challenge and could a competitor use their own IP to block your freedom to operate, potentially preventing the product being exploited and as a result, diminishing the value of the IP rights. The question of whether there is any prior art poses many issues, it is impossible to prove that something does not exist, but a thorough search gives some confidence to mitigate the risk. If there are gaps in the IP due diligence process, potential purchasers or licensees will require warranties or indemnities to protect their investment and minimize the risk as the aim of the due diligence is to minimise the chance of defects and the transaction falling through (Bainbridge and Howell 2014).

4.1 How Does IP Generate Revenue?

Intellectual property rights grant the owner a monopoly right for a set period; this allows the owner to make commercial gain from their innovation in return for sharing it. In practice, for example, the existence of a patented breakthrough product can give a business a head start over their competition. The improvement of existing products or brand recognition can give a business the edge and allow them to charge a premium cost on their IP protected products. Intellectual property, as it states, is a property. It is an asset of the owners, to do with as they wish. Unless using IP to create brand value or using the monopoly to develop a market share a business may decide to sell or license their assets.

Franchising is a version of licensing where the owner provides support and the rights to use certain assets to anyone who can pay the fee and agrees to the terms. Subway®, McDonalds® and Europcar® are all examples of franchising business models. Businesses can also use IP to cross license, allowing competitors to use their assets in return for the right to use the competitors assets, and gain access to other technology that may otherwise cost money, or even be inaccessible.

Looking at the international route, when and if a business decides to expand beyond the national level of protection, IP rights can be vital to ensure the business can have access to the wider market and assert its IP rights. Having the appropriate rights can help to gain key partners in the countries that a business is looking to trade in or establish a foothold in the market (UK IPO).

5 IP Valuation Approach

There are costs involved at all stages of the IP cycle and as such business are becoming more aware of the need to value their IP. The cost element of IP begins at the development stage and achieves full life cycle stage by acquisition. Factoring in the cost of IP generation, allows business to bring the cost of IP rights onto the balance sheet as it can account for development costs at a capitalization stage and businesses can spread the investment made in some IP assets over the expected period of benefit, although there are many restrictions and limitations. For the acquisition stage, accounting rules are required to quantify the value of the assets after a business has been bought, as the acquirer has to decide what it paid for the registered IP assets, and unregistered hidden assets such as goodwill. Several challenges arise because of valuation rules, for example, the value of core assets may seem to be going down, when it may in fact they may be going up. Accurate, regular review of IP value and auditing avoid having a situation where IP assets appear on the balance sheet at a point of sale and as an exit strategy only due to the difference in rules between accounting for development and accounting for acquisitions. (Brassell 2022).

Valuing IP is not as easy as tangible assets and as such requires a valuation method that is suitable and relevant to the industry the business operates in. Intellectual property rights change in value for a variety of reasons and a regular periodic review of IP rights can help quantify the current value of the rights. For example, the worth of a brand name can vary significantly after years of marketing, likewise a protected patent can only hold value and generate revenue if the product stays relevant and avoids becoming redundant. A patent can start with compelling potential and begin its life as a unique solution to a problem, but in time other solutions to the problem may be found which reduce its worth. Alternatively, successfully marketing your product can ensure your patent is very valuable. Trade marks generally gain value as they become better known. The stage of development of the IPR, the availability of information and the aim of the valuation all have a bearing on the method used and each will be discussed next (UK IPO).

There are three main standardised approaches that are used in intellectual property valuation, it is currently not a regulated field, therefore different valuation experts have different approaches (Calboli and Montagnani 2021). The following approaches that are used for intellectual property valuations are provided by the UK IPO as income based, cost method and market value based.

5.1 The Cost Method

The cost method is a value estimate and is cost adjusted for depreciation and obsolescence. It is based on the aim of establishing the value of an IP asset by calculating the cost of developing an identical or similar asset either internally or externally. The cost method poses two fundamental questions. First, how much would it cost to reproduce a given set of assets, taking into account the full cycle of asset production from research and development to acquisition. Second, how much would it cost to replace a given set of assets and it is within these constraints that the cost method values IP assets. The method attempts to determine the value of an IP asset at a particular point of time by aggregating the direct expenditures and opportunity costs involved in its development and mitigating for redundant IP assets. Costs can include labour, materials and equipment, research and development, overheads for utilities, accommodation and support staff, creating a prototype, testing and trials, regulatory approval, certification, and registering the IP asset.

To reiterate, the more detail the IP audit, the more significant the bearing it has on the cost method and what a potential buyer can expect to pay for avoiding the same costs, instead opting to buy the IP assets. Valuable benefits that can make the cost method more attractive is the saving of time for the purchaser, quantifiable expenditure which reflects the cost of attempting to recreate the same IP, and there is already a track record of success with the IP assets. Most importantly, the IP assets are already protected which not only limits other options but also prevents IP protection for the similar assets given the remedies available against infringement. This method of valuing intellectual property assets lends itself to an overall assessment when buying a business. However, as the emphasis is on costs, rather than profit, it can skew the figures so that market potential is not fully appreciated. The cost method does not take account of future value and therefore loses out on a standard by which value is traditionally calculated.

The approach of calculating replacement costs for IP asset with an equivalent asset of similar use and function, can be used more reliably when considering a going concern and solvent valuation. The corresponding IP audit would need to have detailed information relating to the full value historic costs, which evidences the cost of the IP assets, including those still in development. Intellectual Property assets that have future value and are expected to provide an economic benefit, are better suited to the income-based approach, which is considered next (Calboli and Montagnani 2021).

5.2 The Income or Economic Benefit Method

The income-based approach can be a very useful method as it values the revenue the IP assets can generate based on the amount of economic benefit that the intangible asset is predicted to make, adjusted to its present-day value. It is a popular method that anticipates the costs and benefits over the expected lifespan reliable and incorporates externally verified market information. The net profit value is the sum of the difference between benefits, less costs, with an allowance for the discount rate. This method of valuation is based on an assessment of likely future events and is used to consider investments based on whether the net profit value is positive or negative. Central to the income based method is what contribution do the IP assets make to current and future sales or profits, what are the cost savings that can be attributed to specific assets and what is the discount rate to take account of how the money spent could have been made otherwise. Calculating the net profit value is complex. Estimating the economic life of the IP assets over many years requires an estimation of the benefit year on year, with appropriate weighting depending upon the industry. The weighting of the benefit of a pharmaceutical drug will be weighted to the end of the patent whereas fast fashion is much more near term loaded. Therefore, an assessment of how the value and benefit will vary over time is needed as value from IP can be hard to isolate, future projections can be uncertain, especially if market traction is limited. On the plus side, it is a strong incentive for investors to purchase IP assets that have potential as if the expected future IP value is positive, it can be a very attractive investment.

There are several factors that impact on the income based approach, such as, the strength of the IP assets, market size, the industry, the nature of the competition, changes in the economic climate and the cost of registering, enforcing and defending the IP assets. The way in which the IP assets are exploited, the costs involved, the time it will take to get to market and the risks involved all influence this method. A sub method of the income or economic benefit method is the relief from royalties method and is based on an assessment of what royalty costs a company is avoiding by virtue of owning the IP.

Alternatively, the relief from royalties can act as a security for borrowing money from lenders. In 1997, David Bowie issued a 10-year asset-backed bond on the value of his future royalties from publishing rights and master recordings from 25 pre-recorded albums and raised US$55 million. The purchaser received the right to future royalties from the albums until the principal plus 8% annual interest had been repaid (WIPO 2016). Securitisation allows a business to bundle IP assets and lend against predictable future cash flows directly attributable to the IP. The loan size can be determined by the net present value of the expected future profits and gives a manageable discounted cash flow approach, that is adjusted to reflect the risk. There are also opportunities to utilize IP assets as collateral, this is usually relevant to underwrite a recovery value, with a discount rate for going concern expectations (Inngot 2022).

5.3 The Market Value Approach

The market approach is based on a comparison of the actual price paid for a similar IP asset under comparable circumstances, such as, previous transactions. Using this approach for IP valuation can be challenging as assets tend to be unique and novel by nature, and the accuracy of the valuation involves an analysis of the market, an exchange of IP assets, or a group of comparable or similar assets, and where the assets are not comparable, variables are essential to control for the differences. The key advantage to the market approach is that it mirrors tangible asset financing by quantifying the value of the IP assets from prior factual transactions. The business doesn't have to put its assets on sale to work out what people will pay. Rather, the approach examines whether comparable assets have been sold in the market, followed by analysing data on how many businesses, owning comparable assets, have been sold and whether the investment data reveals how much businesses owning comparable assets are worth and what is the licensing agreements value on these assets (Calboli and Montagnani 2021).

Therefore, calculating the value of IP assets by reviewing the sale or licensing of similar products in the market can act as a benchmark for estimating the value of a product based on its existing track record in the market. However, in practice, finding publicly published data on IP transactions, is very difficult as there is no legal requirement to make such data publicly available and therefore, finding relevant data that can be a source for a market approach, is very difficult. Even where there is publicly shared data or a bilateral sharing agreement, the market approach can still be fairly broad as very few IP transactions will provide a valid comparison. The IP assets may differ on exclusivity rights, territorial differences, market conditions, payment structures and the value from specialist support.

Of the three, it is the most difficult approach to apply to all of a company's IP assets as it isn't suitable for all types of IP. For example, a patent is granted for a new or novel invention. Finding comparable information for a novel invention, by its own description, will be a challenge and an objective standard is applied to create financial projections that can still reflect the market value through consumer analysis data. For other IP assets, such as copyright, the market approach method is very effective as royalty rates in each market sector, can be benchmarked as high, medium or low (UK IPO).

5.4 Exploiting Your IP

Exploiting the IP a business owns can create new economic revenue and achieve other strategic goals through commercialization. IP assets can be listed on the company accounts and can be a commodity that is bought, licensed, franchised, or sold. IP assets can be used to secure funding from banks and lenders, as a fixed or floating charge, depending upon the relevant IP due diligence and audit checks as to who controls the asset. The main feature to establishing a valid fixed charge over an IP asset is giving the lender control over the asset. For registered IP assets, with appropriate provisions in the security documentation, such as documenting the security and lender control on the relevant IP register. If there are no control mechanisms in place, the security will instead be potentially granted as a floating charge (Popple 2020).

There are several options to IP commercialization from assignment, licensing, franchising, collaborations, joint ventures, diversification, sponsorship and negotiated access to technology with third parties. Assignment is the most straight forward option as by selling the IP asset, the business is selling all of the attached rights to the IP. Assignment can generate immediate cash and the business is no longer in control of the IP right, and as a result would be infringing their own IP creation by using it, post assignment, without a license.

Under a license agreement, the licensee and licensor are contractually bound to a set of permissions offered to the licensee for an agreed price to the licensor. According to Licensing International's Annual Global Licensing Survey, global sales revenue generated by licensed merchandise and services grew to $315.5 billion in 2021, and global industry royalty revenues reached $17.4 billion. Through a license, an IP owner contractually enters into a legally binding agreement with the licensee and grants the licensee rights to exploit some or all aspects of a particular IP asset. In return, the licensor normally receives compensation as consideration, or a combination of compensation and equity in a business. The purpose of licenses is to create the optimal opportunities to exploit the IP assets, and make the most efficient use of the IP, increasing the economic value and profit that can collectively be achieved by the license agreements (Contreras 2022).

Licensing can be attractive for several reasons, not least of all because of the size of the industry. Often, the licensee has established markets and suppliers, companies can licence-in and there is no transfer of ownerships as the IP ownership is still retained by the licensor. It can also be advantageous over franchising agreements as once the transaction is complete, the level of involvement for the licensor is minimal. There can be upfront payments as well as royalties without losing all rights to the use of the IP asset and is commonly associated to research collaborations with direct access to funds and equipment. Licensing agreements can lead to good links to commercial collaborators and access to markets where the licensee has experience and means of penetrating the market. The licensor still has control as once the license has expired, the full control over the IP asset is back with the licensor.

5.5 IP Financing and Emerging Technologies

As the space inhabited by artificial intelligence continues to grow and transcend aspects of intellectual property creation, there could be room for AI-assisted and AI-generated systems to add to the IP audit and IP valuation methods. As discussed earlier, there are three standardized methods of IP valuation, each with its own advantages and disadvantages. Emerging technologies can assist with both the auditing and valuation systems and help address the different priorities and approaches. AI systems can be developed to enhance IP valuation, overcome buyer and seller disincentives. For the seller, there will be concerns that once core assets are sold, the remaining assets may not be of interest or if the IP is all sold to another business, what will be left of the company. Alternatively, for the buyer, concern can arise over how sustainable the IP assets are or do they rely on a specialist team and it can be difficult to decide on what the value is without comparable transactions. In order to evaluate the role AI systems can play in IP financing, the broader legal landscape pertaining to data to creating common data spaces in the IP industry, from which to generate more accurate IP comparable data and support IP financing and lending (Williams 2022). For AI, there is potential to overcome its challenges around ethics and trustworthiness and create AI assisted and or generated valuation methods. The UK IPO offers an IP finance toolkit which acts as a guide for businesses and supports their IP audit before applying for an IP backed loan or financing. To further support IP management and commercialisation strategies, as well as raise awareness of finance options available, toolkits can be useful however AI systems that can address the limitations with current valuation processes.

6 In Conclusion: IP Financing for Businesses

IP audits can be very insightful and relevant to a company's financial forecast and value. The audit will establish whether the appropriate IP policies and procedures are in place and what IP rights, a company has. The more detailed and accurate, the more reliable the audit is, in terms of validity and status. The key priority of the audit varies from the identification of the most valuable assets and the associated product lines, as well as how well they are properly protected. The IP audit is periodically reviewed to account for licences, terms and conditions, pending actions and legal proceedings. Cost of development of IP rights is the only way to bring IP assets onto the balance sheet. The audit will establish whether the appropriate IP policies and procedures are in place, and record registered or unregistered assets, their validity and status. The audit aims to identify the most valuable rights as core assets. IP due diligence is critical for identifying and verifying IP assets and liabilities, in relation to an IP transaction.

The IP audit and due diligence of all relevant IP assets, including registered assets such as patents and trademarks and also unregistered assets that include copyright, trade secrets and know-how, all contribute to the valuation of a company. To fully exploit the IP a business owns, the three different valuation methods monetise IP and generate revenue. For the cost approach, the valuation method quantifies the reproduction cost of a given set of assets from inception to production and what the cost of replacing the IP assets would be. As a methos, this is the most straightforward reflection of the investment made by the business in terms of tangible data from the cost of human capital, direct costs, overheads, and other ancillary costs to create a cost-based valuation of the IP assets. The main disadvantage is that although cost does reflect the investment made and the skill, labour and capital that has been spent on creating the IP assets, that doesn't necessarily mirror the value and therefore is often the least attractive of the valuation methods.

The market value method is focussed on the comparable value of the assets. This is an analysis of both comparable assets that have been sold on the market and the sale of businesses owning comparable assets. The market value method relies more on investment data on the IP value and ancillary licensing agreements. Despite this method having the most resemblance to tangible asset valuation, it is flawed as the market comparison of intangibles are not as readily available as physical property. The final method of income-based valuations is the most popular of the three methods as it assesses the value of the IP assets based on current and future profits. On the other hand, it is uncertain and can be difficult to mitigate the risk, if the market traction is limited. To further complicate matters, valuation priorities are different for each approach and depends on the purpose of the IP audit such as securitisation, collateral, licensing, franchising, or equity financing. AI can play a very important role in the development of AI-assisted and AI-generated audit and valuation methods to expand the current market limitations on ascertaining the most accurate value of IP assets and creating more opportunities for IP financing and lending.

References

Bainbridge, D and Howell, C. Intellectual Property Asset Management : How to Identify, Protect, Manage and Exploit Intellectual Property Within the Business Environment, (2014), Routledge.

Brassell, M. Challenges in harnessing IP for finance, (2022), Inngot Limited.

Calboli, I. and Montagnani, M. Handbook of Intellectual Property Research: Lenses, Methods, and Perspectives (2021), Oxford University Press.

Contreras, J. Introduction to Intellectual Property Licensing. In Intellectual Property Licensing and Transactions: Theory and Practice, (2022), Cambridge University Press.

Copyright, Design and Patents Act, 1988

Durant, I. Unlocking potential of intellectual property rights to support the creative economy, (2021), United Nations Conference on Trade and Development.

Millien, R. The use of competitive intelligence in IP monetisation, (2014), Intellectual Asset Management.

Patent Act 1977

Popple, L. Security over IP. Considerations when taking security over IP, (2020), Taylor Wessing.

Singh, J. How startups and SMEs should think about IP: an investor's perspective, (2021), WIPO Magazine.
Tang, D. Inaugural High-level Conversation on Unlocking Intangible Asset Finance, (2022), World Intellectual Property Office.
Trade Mark Act 1994
UK Intellectual Property Office
UK Intellectual Property Office (UK IPO), IP Finance Toolkit, (2014). Available at IP Finance Toolkit (publishing.service.gov.uk).
Williams, L. Anonos Secures $50 Million in IP-Backed Financing to Deliver Data Privacy Technology with 100% Accuracy and Utility to Data-Driven Enterprises, (2022), Business Wire.
World Intellectual Property Office, (WIPO), Methodology for the Development of National Intellectual Property Strategies, (2016). Available at https://www.wipo.int/edocs/pubdocs/en/wipo_pub_958_3.pdf
World Intellectual Property Office, (2021), Unlocking IP-backed Financing: Country Perspectives. Singapore's Jouney. Geneva: WIPO.

Transformative (Bio)technologies in Knowledge Societies: Of Patents and Intellectual Commons

Mariela de Amstalden and Nivita Sukhadia

1 Transformative Biotechnologies: Cell-Cultivation for Human Food Consumption

The year was 1931. In a line perhaps more suitable to science fiction writing at the time, Winston Churchill envisioned cell-based meats by declaring that: "[w]e shall escape the absurdity of growing a whole chicken in order to eat the breast or wing, by growing these parts separately under a suitable medium" (Churchill 1931). Arguably, a technology, and the products it produces, is only disruptive when it reaches the masses. Promoted as a more sustainable alternative to conventional proteins, research into cell-cultivation technology for human food consumption (cellular agriculture) has gained new urgency in response to pressing

M. de Amstalden (✉)
Law School, University of Exeter, Exeter, UK
e-mail: M.De-Amstalden@exeter.ac.uk

N. Sukhadia
University of Cambridge, Faculty of Law Cambridge, Exeter, UK

N. Naim (ed.), *Developments in Intellectual Property Strategy*,
https://doi.org/10.1007/978-3-031-42576-9_8

global challenges. In essence, these products are produced by tissue and bioprocess engineering that result in a product that is molecularly identical to conventional agricultural ones, like meat.

In light of this, some initial regulatory activity with the aim of accommodating (or hindering) the placing on the market of such products could be identified in different jurisdictions, most notably in Singapore -the first country to grant regulatory approval for cell-cultivated meats. Nonetheless, the regulatory pushback from established global market players in the meat, fish and diary industries is noticeable. For cell-cultivation food companies, their new products provide the most efficient answer to reduce greenhouse gas emissions, feed a growing world population and prevent food-borne diseases. For conventional producers of food, cellular agriculture products are artificial and thus, not equivalent. In our highly intertwined global food supply chain, biotechnological advances tend to precede existing rules-based regulation, challenging the effective responsiveness of a valid legal framework. I have argued elsewhere that the language used within the law will thus undoubtedly have social, economic, political and cultural consequences for the future of food systems (de Amstalden 2021), but also for future global governance mechanisms (de Amstalden 2016).

Conversely, decades of industrialised animal farming have significantly contributed to anthropogenic climate change. Livestock-based meat production limits the use of scarce natural resources like water and land, while also releasing large amounts of Greenhouse Gas (GHG) emissions. The amount of animal protein required to feed a global population that is expected to reach 9.7 billion in 2050 is likely to double, compounding the severity of implications for the sustainable use of available resources.

While emerging biotechnologies are currently being developed to mitigate the negative effects of livestock-based meat consumption, the lack of a responsive regulatory framework has the potential to stifle innovation, just as uncertainties about likely technical and social outcomes inhibit informed decision-making. Arguably, effective stewardship of cell-cultivation technology products requires broad political and social assessment and engagement.

Intellectual Property Rights (IPRs) have been inextricably intertwined with the emergence of transformative technologies as means to reward intellectual creation since the beginning of human ingenuity. Cell-cultivation technology to produce food for human consumption is no exception. From trade secrets to patents and trademarks, the production of food for human consumption using cell-cultivation technology creates a novel scientific field ('cellular agriculture') while confronting innovators, manufacturers, regulators and consumers with an array of challenges. What we understand as IP, and how we engage with it, will shape the contours of academic discourse, inform public policy debates determine entrepreneurial success and challenge consumer perceptions. Encountering IP law at a multiplicity of levels, cellular agriculture as an emerging field of (legal) enquiry that appears to challenge Lockean approaches to IP as a legal monopoly, questioning their limits to promote social progress.

2 Saving the Intellectual Commons in Future Knowledge Societies

By its very nature, transformative biotechnologies confront the law with an array of issues, from responses to risks in light of scientific uncertainty, labelling and consumer protection, restrictions on international trade and investment to intellectual property limitations. I posit here that we lack a holistic understanding of the nature, causes and implications of regulatory shifts that suitably address transformative biotechnologies like cell-cultivation in ever-expanding knowledge societies.

Future knowledge is contingent upon past forms thereof (Dupre and Somsen 2019). However, whereas productivity has played an essential role in traditional societies during the industrial age, knowledge is the designated vector that generates social and economic results nowadays (Drucker 1993). While this paradigm shift appeared long undisputed (Cerroni 2020), it has been posited that the encoding of knowledge in law precipitates a new knowledge capitalism that is particularly evident in patent law as a fiction that limits cognitive processes with symbolic capital (Stehr 2022). Today, IPRs are closely linked to a productivist paradigm that rewards efficient extraction of value-generating activity over the creation of public welfare in its many facets. In this vein, the commons are constitutive of a foundational element in capitalist intellectual production (Broumas 2017), while potentially catapulting nonrivalry in intellectual goods (Bracha 2018).

A flourishing innovation ecosystem is necessarily attuned to scientific endeavours. Growing calls for open science as a form of co-creation may find refuge in knowledge commons phenomena that emphasise their role in scientific enquiry (Ranganathan 2016). Equally, large sets of information ('big data') have generated significant options for open science and the formation of knowledge societies (Wessels et al. 2017). As such, there are alternatives to innovation incentives that purely rely on legal monopolies -as it is mostly the case with various regulatory approaches to IPRs. For example, IP self-regulation has been considered as a basis for user generated law in knowledge societies (Riis 2016), that is, a bottom-up approach to regulation by IP.

With the aim of gaining a better understanding of 'knowledge society' epistemologies, I explore below the role of patents in cellular agriculture, a field of enquiry that uses cell-cultivation technology, as a case study to elucidate the extent to which IP rights can be deployed to generate optimal public welfare while conserving and indeed expanding spheres of intellectual commons, understood as the abstract embodiment of shared resources available for all.

3 Patent Effectiveness and the WTO TRIPS

Arguably, the effectiveness of a patent is determined by its term of protection. Art. 33 TRIPS, in establishing a period of twenty years, significantly boosts the strength of patent protection under the law of the World Trade Organisation (WTO law). This is particularly true for fields of technology where long-term research precedes the production of a marketable invention, such cell-cultivation. Although today's technology tends to become obsolete more rapidly as the average period of useful life attributed to it by society decreases (Pires de Carvalho 2010), the average lifespan of patents continues to correspond with the cycles of Schumpeter's "creative destruction" (Schumpeter 1947).

In setting the term of patent protection under TRIPS, Art. 33 does not provide for any distinction on the basis of the field of technology, or extent of exploitation, of patented inventions. Such distinctions would arguably encourage discrimination among technological fields, leading to an ad absurdum scenario whereby patent protection would be assigned on a case-by-case basis, leading to extreme legal uncertainty (Pires de Carvalho 2010).

Art. 33 stipulates that "[t]he term of protection available shall not end before the expiration of a period of twenty years counted from the filing date." The term of a patent may not be shorter than 20 years, even if the actual effects of the patent do not occur until after its grant. Accordingly, Art. 33 identifies the earliest possible date for the end of patent protection. Although the provision ties the patent term to the date of filing and does not contain specific regulations relating to the calculation of time limits, this aspect was clarified by the Appellate Body in Canada— Patent Term. In its view, the calculation of a term of patent protection is determined by taking the date of filing of the patent application and adding twenty years (AB Canada – Patent Term, para. 85). Conversely, Members are not bound to compensate for delays, for instance, in the examination process of the application or in the marketing approval of products (Correa 2022). As a result, the national patent regulations of Members remain decisive. However, patent protection may not be significantly curtailed by unreasonable delays in the procedures for granting patents, as such delays are inconsistent with the obligations under Art. 62.1 and 2 TRIPS.

More specifically, the Panel in Canada—Patent Term found that Art. 33 establishes a minimum term of protection for patents, which also raised questions about the possibility of extending rights and obligations even after the expiry of said patent terms, which would generate spillover effects (Canada – Patent Term, paras 6.57-6.121). The Panel Report was subsequently appealed and, relying on the availability requirement in Art. 33, the Appellate Body considered the provision "straightforward" in stipulating that the filing date plus 20 years is the earliest date on which the term of protection of a patent may end and that this 20-year term must be "a readily discernible and specific right, and it must be clearly seen as such by the patent applicant when a patent application is filed"

(AB Canada-Patent Term, paras 84 et seq.). On that basis, the Appellate Body rejected Canada's defensive argument, according to which other statutory and regulatory provisions would allow patent applicants to delay the procedure so as to extend the patent term to one de facto equivalent to the term laid down in Art. 33 (AB Canada-Patent Term, paras 94 et seq.). It held that:

> The opportunity to obtain a twenty-year patent term must not be 'available' only to those who are somehow able to meander successfully through a maze of administrative procedures. The opportunity [...] must be a readily discernible and specific right, and it must be clearly seen as such by the patent applicant when a patent application is filed (AB Canada – Patent Term, para. 92).

Thus, in view of the Appellate Body's understanding, Art. 33 does not support an "equivalence test" whereby a combination of procedures, when used in a particular sequence, may add up to twenty years.

Art. 33 does not, however, regulate further terms of protection existing independently of a patent, such as supplementary protection certificates (SPCs). The legitimacy of SPCs can be derived from Art. 33, which only determines the earliest possible date for the end of patent protection. If the patent itself may remain in force longer, this must hold true also for SPCs after the expiry of the patent term. Art. 1.1, sentence 2 supports this interpretation. However, Art. 33 only relates to the patent protection itself. Accordingly, supplementary protection may not be deducted from the lifetime of the patent. The protection by the patent itself shall not end before the expiry of the time limit specified in Art. 33. This is also applicable if the gradual interaction of the patent and supplementary protection operates such that the invention will be protected like a patent at least until the expiry of such time. Art. 33 thus outlaws situations where the protection of a patent itself would end before the expiry of the 20 years and then be substituted by supplementary protection. There is no general requirement in TRIPS to conduct substantive examinations of patent applications.16 However, it is Members' obligation to put in place a scrutinizing mechanism that assesses whether a claimed invention complies with the mandatory conditions of patentability under Arts. 27.1

and 29.1 TRIPS. This requirement also applies to the re-registration of foreign patents.

I have argued elsewhere (de Amstalden 2021) that while regulatory transparency requirements can be transformative, it is not the only factor with the potential to play a beneficial role in the shift from intensive agricultural practices to more efficient, sustainable biotechnologies. Patents are designed to promote invention and innovation by granting patent holders a comprehensive competitive advantage against third party imitation in return for public disclosure of information about the invention (Granstrand 2019). It is crucial to recognise that there are critical public transparency implications associated with patents. Misconceptions about IP rights, and patents in particular, have led the general public to believe that patents hide information from third parties. Quite to the contrary, a patent cannot be successfully filed without an accurate disclosure of its inventiveness. Public disclosure of information is the price to pay in return for a time-limited monopoly, essentially to recover research and development investment. As such, the protection afforded by patents is not confidentiality – as it is the case with trade secrets- but an exclusive right to use the invention and license the technology if so desired. Through this lens, market action relying on trade secrets as the main IP strategy would indeed run contrary to increasingly robust calls for 'open science' in cellular agriculture, for it is precisely the confidentiality demanded by trade secrets that considerably hinders technological development behind closed (and locked) doors.

Specifically for novel foods, patenting processes -as opposed to products- tend to be less stringent, as the patentability requirements of novelty and inventiveness are easier to meet. Patents also afford the benefits of awarding credibility, as well as the basis for licensing of technologies. In fast-paced technological fields, as it is the case with cellular agriculture, the term of protection conferred by patents is an attractive alternative that warrants the (at times onerous) filing procedures. It is telling that the last years saw a significant increase in the number of patent applications in the cellular agriculture sector (Ng et al. 2021). Arguably, this development may be explained via a number of reasons, which are potentially two sides of the same coin. First, companies had no incentive to date to file for patent applications earlier to conserve their technological advantage over competitors through trade secrets law via enforceable confidentiality agreements, as we have seen previously. Secondly, companies could have been incentivised by venture capitalists to file for patents in order to successfully secure capital for expansion. Being mindful of the divergent promissory narratives in cellular agriculture discourse (de Amstalden 2021; Stephens et al. 2019), it is also conceivable that reluctance to publicise the obtention of patents in the cellular agriculture sector is connected to the potential for consumer confusion and the reinforcement of perceptions about the 'unnaturalness' of the novel foods.

4 Conclusion

This chapter explored the impact of transformative biotechnologies like cell-cultivation on ever-expanding knowledge societies. In doing so, it examined the role of patents, and their terms of protection under international IP law to elucidate whether and to what extent IPR as conceived today are compatible with the calls for open science and the solidification of an intellectual commons.

Just as cell-cultivation technology has the potential to be considered a 'technology of abundance', IP rights can, and indeed, should be construed as an abundant resource. In doing so, it demonstrated, with patents as an example, that IP rights have the ability to invigorate multiple tonalities in new global economic governance mechanisms, while being mindful of, and in fact amplify, a variety of seemingly unrelated elements uniting to address complex social challenges. Whether IP rights as public interest mechanisms succeed in advancing policy considerations to reimagine food systems through cellular agriculture merits further empirical research.

References

(Maidana-Eletti) de Amstalden, Mariela (2016), Global Food Governance: Implications of Food Safety and Quality Standards in International Trade Law, Peter Lang Publishers.

Bracha, Oren (2018), Give Us Back Our Tragedy: Nonrivalry in Intellectual Property Law and Policy, 19 Theoretical Enquiries in Law, 633.

Broumas, Antonios (2017), The Ontology of the Intellectual Commons, International Journal of Communication 11, 1507–1527

Cerroni, Andrea (2020), Understanding the Knowledge Society: A New Paradigm in the Sociology of Knowledge, Edward Elgar 2020.

Correa, Carlos (2022), Interpreting the Flexibilities Under the TRIPS Agreement, Springer.

De Amstalden, Mariela (2021), Seafood without the Sea, 23 Journal of World Trade and Investment 1, 68–94.

Drucker, Peter F. (1993) "The rise of the knowledge society." The Wilson Quarterly, vol. 17, no. 2, spring 1993, pp. 52 et seq.

Dupré, S. and Somsen, G. (2019). The History of Knowledge and the Future of Knowledge Societies. Berichte zur Wissenschaftsgeschichte, 42, 186–199. https://doi.org/10.1002/bewi.201900006

Granstrand, O. (2019). Patents and policies for innovations and entrepreneurship. In: Takenaka, T. (Ed), Research Handbook on Patent Law and Theory, Edward Elgar, 55–86.

Neil Stephens, Alexandra Sexton, Clemens Driessen, 'Making Sense of Making Meat: Key Moments in the First 20 Years of Tissue Engineering Muscle to Make Food', Frontiers in Sustainable Food Systems, Volume 3 - 2019. https://doi.org/10.3389/fsufs.2019.00045

Ng, E., Singh, S., Yap, W., Tay, S., Choudhury, D., 2021. Cultured meat: a patentometric analysis. Critical Reviews in Food Science and Nutrition, https://doi.org/10.1080/10408398.2021.1980760.

Pires de Carvalho, Nunes (2010), The Trips Regime of Patent Rights, 3rd Edition, Wolters Kluwer.

Ranganathan, Surabhi (2016), Global Commons, European Journal of International Law, 27(3), 693–717.

Riis, Thomas (2016), User Generated Law: Re-Constructing Intellectual Property Knowledge in the Knowledge Society, Edward Elgar.

Schumpeter, Joseph (1947), The Creative Response in Economic History, 7 The Journal of Economic History 2, November 1947, pp. 149 – 159.

Stehr, Nico (2022), Knowledge Capitalism, Routledge.

Wessels, Bridgette, Finn, Rachel, Sveinsdottir, Thordis and Wadhwa, Kush (2017) Open Data and the Knowledge Society', Amsterdam University

Winston Churchill, 'Fifty Years Hence', The Strand Magazine (December 1931).

Correction to: Fostering Innovation by Utilising Big Data: The Data Act and the Risk of Quasi-Exclusivity Reinforcing Data Lockups

Marc A. Stuhldreier

Correction to:

Chapter 2 in: N. Naim (ed.), *Developments in Intellectual Property Strategy*, https://doi.org/10.1007/978-3-031-42576-9_2

The chapter "Fostering Innovation by Utilising Big Data: The Data Act and the Risk of Quasi-Exclusivity Reinforcing Data Lockups", written by Marc A. Stuhldreier, was originally published electronically on the publisher's internet portal without open access. With the author(s)' decision to opt for Open Choice, the copyright of the chapter has been changed on 14-July-2023 to © 2024 The Author(s), under exclusive license to Springer Nature Switzerland AG 2024 and the chapter is forthwith distributed under a Creative Commons Attribution **Open Access** This chapter is licensed under the terms of the Creative Commons Attribution

The updated version of this chapter can be found at https://doi.org/10.1007/978-3-031-42576-9_2

N. Naim (ed.), *Developments in Intellectual Property Strategy*,
https://doi.org/10.1007/978-3-031-42576-9_9

 Funded by: Linköpings Universitet

Correction to: An Artificial Intelligence Invention Protection Model

Budi Agus Riswandi and Galih Dwi Ramadhan

Correction to:
Chapter 5 in: N. Naim (ed.), *Developments in Intellectual Property Strategy*. https://doi.org/10.1007/978-3-031-42576-9_5

Chapter 5 was inadvertently published listing Budi Agus Riswandi as the sole author. But this chapter was coauthored by Galih Dwi Ramadhan, and both the contributors are now listed as authors in the revised version. The biography of the coauthor Galih Dwi Ramadhan is now added to the notes on contributors section.

In addition to the above, we have removed the biography of Abdurrahman Alfaqiih and Dodik Setiawan Nur Heriyanto since they have not contributed to this book.

The updated version of this chapter can be found at
https://doi.org/10.1007/978-3-031-42576-9_5

N. Naim (ed.), *Developments in Intellectual Property Strategy*,
https://doi.org/10.1007/978-3-031-42576-9_10

Annexure: Table of Cases

CLM v CLN [2022] SGHC 46
Coca-Cola v Barr
Countess Housewares v Addis
Infopaq International A/S v Danske Dagbaldes Forening C- 5/08
IRC v Muller & Co's Margarine Ltd [1901]
Janesh s/o Rajkumar v Unknown Person [2022]
National Provincial Bank Ltd v Ainsworth [1965]
Osbourne v Persons Unknown [2022]
Ruscoe v Cryptopia Ltd (in liq) [2020]
Sheraton Corp. of America v Sheraton Motels [1964]
Strix Ltd v Otter Controls Ltd [1995]
Thaler v Comptroller General of Patents Trade Marks And Designs [2021] EWCA Civ 1374
Thaler v Commissioner of Patents [2021] FCA 879
Visual Entidad De Gestion De Artistas Plasticos/ Punto Fa, S.L. [2022] AJM B 1900/2022 – ECLI:ES: JMB: 2022:1900

N. Naim (ed.), *Developments in Intellectual Property Strategy*,
https://doi.org/10.1007/978-3-031-42576-9

Index

N. Naim (ed.), *Developments in Intellectual Property Strategy*,
https://doi.org/10.1007/978-3-031-42576-9

22332402

The manufacturer's authorised representative in the EU is Springer Nature Customer Service Centre GmbH, Europaplatz 3, 69115 Heidelberg, Germany. If you have any concerns regarding our products, please contact ProductSafety@springernature.com

Printed and bound by CPI Group (UK) Ltd, Croydon, CR0 4YY

28/09/2026

02224083-0002